by Nancie McDermott

QUICK & EASY VIETNAMESE

75 EVERYDAY RECIPES

PHOTOGRAPHS *BY* CAREN ALPERT

CHRONICLE BOOKS

Library of Congress Cataloging-in-Publication Data available.

ISBN 0-8118-4434-X

Manufactured in China.

Designed by **Jay Peter Salvas**
Prop styling by **Peggi Jeung**
Food styling by **Basil Friedman**
Photo Assistant **David Turek**
Assistant Food Stylist **Victoria Woollard**
This book was typeset in **Perpetua 11/13, Gill Sans 9/13, and Formata**
The photographer wishes to thank **James Henderson and Joe Macaluso**

Distributed in Canada by Raincoast Books
9050 Shaughnessy Street
Vancouver, British Columbia V6P 6E5

10 9 8 7 6 5 4 3 2 1

Chronicle Books LLC
85 Second Street
San Francisco, California 94105

www.chroniclebooks.com

To my father, James Patrick McDermott, a magnificent, generous, brave, intelligent man, thanks to whom I love to read, travel, share, laugh, and linger at the table with family and friends.

TABLE OF CONTENTS

INTRODUCTION

From its craggy northernmost border with China to the lush paddy fields and coconut plantations of the Mekong Delta, Vietnam nurtures an extraordinary cuisine. The nation's ancient Chinese heritage has formed a deep foundation for its culinary traditions. The cuisine of Vietnam is unique, however, distinct from that of China and of all its Asian neighbors, with which Vietnam shares so much in terms of climate, geography, and history.

With some 1,400 miles of seacoast, a vast network of rivers, and a sultry tropical climate, Vietnam nurtures vegetables galore, fragrant herbs, and luscious fruit. The Vietnamese kitchen celebrates this bounty with a fresh, delicate approach to food, bright with clear flavors and hearty with shellfish, fish, meat, noodles, and wraps. Simple, unseasoned rice anchors the food of Vietnam in East Asian fashion, but the good things cooked to go with it sparkle with Southeast Asia's edible treasures: lemongrass, ginger, pineapple, and papaya team with fresh cilantro, mint, basil, and chilies to brighten every bite.

Contrasts prevail in Vietnamese cuisine: Sour flavors are balanced by salty ones, and sweet notes are answered by a little heat from ground pepper and chilies. If the fish is fried crisp, the sauce served with it will be a smooth purée. Delicate summer rolls call for a thick and pungent sauce based on salt-preserved soybeans, an edible marriage of heaven and earth. When chicken curry appears on the table, with its velvety, spice-infused coconut sauce, so does its companion dish of lime juice, salt, and pepper, balancing the richness of the curry with clear notes of citrus and heat.

In Vietnam as in most of Asia, soup is a mainstay, served right along with the rice and other dishes, and enjoyed throughout the meal. Neither first course nor entrée, soup is more like a beverage within a typical Western meal. Whether it's a simple broth like Clear Soup with Catfish, Tomatoes, and Fresh Dill (page 45) or the lavish, seafood-laden Sweet and Tangy Soup with Pineapple, Tamarind, and Shrimp (page 48), a bowl of soup provides a little break from the variously flavored dishes on the Vietnamese table.

As in China and East Asia, the Vietnamese eat their rice in bowls with chopsticks. And like these northern neighbors, they enjoy their meals seated around a table. In the rest of Southeast Asia, the way people eat reflects their cultural connections to India. In Thailand, Burma, Cambodia, and Laos, people dine seated on woven mats, eating their rice from a plate with spoons or the fingers of the right hand.

Hu Tieu *Noodles with Pork and Shrimp, Saigon Style; page 131*

Like all their Southeast Asian neighbors, Vietnamese cooks make brilliant use of their country's tropical bounty, from coconut milk, tamarind, and limes, to chilies, green mango, lotus stems, and a staggering array of fragrant and pungent fresh herbs. Vietnam's cuisine veers from the beaten path of Southeast Asian cooking in numerous ways, however. Rather than stir-frying most vegetables with a handful of meat or other protein, cooks in Vietnam tend to let meat be meat and green be green. Vegetables are cooked simply: spinach is fried with garlic, and eggplant is grilled and then topped with a tangy clear sauce. Other vegetables appear raw, cool, crisp, and ready for bundling into lettuce packets or rice wrappers, along with grilled meats, fish or seafood, a tangle of rice noodles, fresh herbs, and a splash of vibrant dipping sauce.

Meat often stands alone, minimally seasoned. It is briefly grilled as kebabs, meatballs, or in thin strips, and is served up with a pungent sauce. Meat and fish are also simmered briefly in a clay pot with fish sauce and sugar to make a *kho* dish, creating lots of delectable sauce to enjoy over rice. What in many places would be one person's serving of chicken, pork, or fish can therefore satisfy many guests. In addition to stretching a little protein to feed more people, a *kho* dish requires a minimum amount of fuel and effort.

The ingredients for cooking Vietnamese food are easy to come by these days in the West. Fish sauce, rice noodles, and rice papers for wraps and rolls can be found in any Asian market, or through the mail-order and Internet sources on page 162. Now that soy sauce, Asian sesame oil, and hoisin sauce are widely available in major supermarkets, you can often buy the condiments you will need for cooking delicious Vietnamese dishes in one trip to your local grocery store. Add some meat, fish, shellfish, or a vegetarian protein source to your shopping cart, along with a big jar of roasted peanuts and a small one of sesame seeds, and then head for the produce section. Toss in some leaf lettuce, limes, carrots, scallions, onions, and garlic. Then top it all off with a bouquet of fresh cilantro or mint, and head for the check-out counter.

Vietnamese cuisine survived more than a century of French colonial presence beautifully, moving into the postcolonial world and now the new millennium with her culinary identity clear and strong. Vietnam's cuisine has remained quite Vietnamese, even while clearing a space for the affectionate adoption of a few worthy French traditions, notably good strong coffee, crème caramel, and baguettes freshly baked every day.

You won't need much in the way of new equipment to cook the quick and easy Vietnamese food featured here. A big deep skillet will work as well as a wok; a good chef's knife will chop as well as an Asian cleaver; and a pair of V-shaped stainless steel tongs will usually stand in nicely for the more traditional cooking chopsticks.

Vietnam's cooking techniques tend to be straightforward and easily translated to a Western kitchen. Grilling is a national pastime. While the practice of marinating meats before grilling is common, the time required tends to be measured in minutes rather than hours.

Noodles rule in Vietnam, and once you get used to the simple basics of cooking them, you will be putting together fine noodle feasts: big, delicious bowls of soup noodles; tasty stir-fries; fast, fresh noodle salads; and countless noodle-centered wrap-it-up meals. These dishes start with a platter of quickly grilled or roasted chicken, pork, beef, salmon, shrimp, tofu, or portobello mushrooms, cooked at home or carried in from the deli. The meat or vegetable is paired with a supply of lettuce cups, or softened rice-paper triangles, aromatic herbs, a tangle of rice noodles, and a bowl or two of brilliantly flavored sauces. Family and friends start picking and choosing, trying this herb and that sauce, relaxing and reviving, almost as though they were playing with their food.

The truth is, playing with food is a way of life in Vietnam. So is making flavor-packed meals quickly and simply, using what you have or can find easily on any given day. Some days I create a culinary masterpiece worthy of an ovation. Most days, though, I have more on my plate than fixing dinner, but I long for something tasty and freshly made, interesting but not too complicated, something I can step away from if the phone rings, or homework issues arise, or the dog begs to go out. I want to make something satisfying, and good enough to make my whole family start to smile. *Quick & Easy Vietnamese* is filled with this kind of food, along with a few dazzlers for the occasional tour de force when you have lots of helping hands.

If you enjoy Vietnamese food already, look up your favorites. If you are new to Vietnamese flavors, browse through the recipes and find something that sounds good. Make a grocery list, drop by the supermarket, and start cooking. You will love the delicate feast of Vietnamese cooking the quick and easy way.

PANTRY NOTES

Here are three pantry lists for you to consider as you begin cooking Vietnamese dishes at home. The A list consists of ingredients used so often that it's worth keeping them on hand. Note that it is quite short, and that most if not all the items are easy to find.

The B list consists of ingredients used frequently in Vietnamese cooking, and therefore well worth stocking if you plan to make this food part of your repertoire. Some are used more than others: Bean sprouts, lemongrass, and sesame oil will be called for more often than star anise, hoisin sauce, and tamarind liquid. No need to track down each and every item. You can acquire what you need as you go through the recipes and pick out dishes you want to cook.

The C list contains ingredients used occasionally and worth having if you want to extend your knowledge of Vietnamese cuisine.

Many ingredients in these lists are ones you know well and may already have on hand. Some will be less familiar, so check the glossary (pages 14–20) for background information if you want to know more. Remember that all the ingredients can be found through the mail-order/Internet sources listed on page 162. You'll probably find most of them in a good Asian market near your home. Or plan a shopping expedition to a nearby metropolis or a community with a large Asian population.

Farmers' markets are a wonderful source for Asian herbs and vegetables, many of them organically grown. They're also the ideal place to buy basic items like tomatoes, cucumbers, lettuce, green onions, herbs, and farm-fresh eggs.

These days, many of the things you need for Vietnamese cooking await you in your nearest well-stocked supermarket or healthfood store. In the last twenty years, an abundance of Asian ingredients that were once obscure have been now widely available around the country. What a gift! This is a grand time to be cooking Vietnamese food.

A-LIST INGREDIENTS

Baguettes
Chili-garlic sauce or dried red chili flakes
Dried rice noodles
Fish sauce
Fresh herbs: cilantro, mint, basil, dill, or a combination
Garlic: heads, peeled whole cloves, or chopped
Green onions
Limes or lemons
Peanuts, roasted and salted
Soy sauce
Standard pantry items: salt, pepper, sugar, vegetable oil, white vinegar, onions, rice, and eggs

B-LIST INGREDIENTS

Aromatic rice: jasmine, basmati, and other naturally fragrant types
Basil: Asian basil (*rau que*) or any other type of basil
Bean sprouts
Bean thread noodles
Caramel sauce
Chilies: fresh, hot green and red ones, from relatively mild jalapeños to tiny, incendiary Thai ones
Chinese dried mushrooms (also called dried shiitakes)
Cilantro
Cinnamon sticks
Cloves
Coconut milk, unsweetened
Coffee: dark roast, such as domestic Café du Monde or imported Trung Nguyên Coffee
Curry powder
Dill
Ginger, fresh, chopped, or puréed
Hoisin sauce
Lemongrass, fresh or frozen
Mint
Mung bean centers
Pineapple, fresh or canned
Rau ram
Rice noodles, fresh or frozen
Rice paper wrappers
Sesame oil: Asian style, toasted and brown
Sesame seeds, white
Shallots
Star anise
Sticky rice, long-grain
Sugarcane, water-packed in 48-ounce cans
Sweetened condensed milk
Tamarind: liquid or pulp, or Indian-style tamarind chutney
Tapioca pearls (small ones)

C-LIST INGREDIENTS

Anchovy paste
Banana leaves (available frozen)
Brown bean sauce (also called fermented soybean paste)
Chinese chives (also called garlic chives)
Oyster sauce
Pickled mustard greens (such as Tiensien preserved vegetable)
Roasted rice powder
Shrimp, dried
Shrimp paste sauce (also called *mam tom* or *mam ruoc*)
Soy sauce, dark
Squid, dried

GLOSSARY OF VIETNAMESE INGREDIENTS

Fresh Herbs for the Vietnamese Kitchen

No cuisine holds fragrant, flavorful herbs in higher esteem than that of Vietnam. The ubiquitous leafy platters of lettuce and herbs that adorn Vietnamese tables at mealtime are a silent affirmation of this truth. Nowhere else is there comparable devotion to sparkling flavors and aromas, nor such dedication to enhancing the pleasure of every bite. Many of the components of these platters, called *dia rau song,* are herbs well-known and easily found in the West: cilantro, mint, basil, and dill, along with green onions, bean sprouts, sliced fresh hot chilies, and chunks of lime. Here is a little herb primer, a field guide to the culinary herbs you are most likely to find in Vietnamese restaurants, grocery stores, and farmers' markets in the West.

ASIAN BASIL *(RAU QUE)*

Asian basil *(Ocimum basilicum)* has a familiar scent to basil-loving cooks in the West, but it looks a bit different from its European cousins. Look for sharp, pointy leaves on purple stems, often adorned with tiny white flowers and purple buds. This herb is also known as Thai basil, and its Thai name is *bai horapah.*

CILANTRO *(RAU NGO)*

A staple of kitchens around the world, cilantro *(Coriandrum sativum)* is also known as fresh coriander and Chinese parsley. Keep cilantro on hand, as you will use it often when cooking Vietnamese food.

CRAB CLAW HERB *(RAU CANG CUA)*

Named for its shape, this less common herb is appreciated for its peppery taste.

DILL *(RAU THI LA)*

Used in Laos and northern Vietnam, the feathery fronds of dill *(Anethum graveolens)* make a delicious and aromatic companion to fish. Its signature use in the cuisine of Vietnam is in *Cha Ca* Fish with Fresh Dill, Hanoi Style (page 89), the famed northern dish made with catfish, turmeric, and handfuls of dill.

FISH MINT *(RAU DIEP CA)*

Enjoyed in salads and wraps, this leaf *(Houthuynia cordata)* has little fragrance but provides a powerful sour note. The shape of *rau diep ca's* leaves earns it an additional common name of fish-scale mint.

GREEN PERILLA *(RAU KINH GIOI)*

This flavorful light-green leaf *(Elsholtzia ciliata)*, bears a visual resemblance to perilla, and hence its common name. It is actually a cousin to lemon balm. In Vietnam, it shows up among the abundant leafy herbs presented with soups.

MINT *(RAU HUNG LUI)*

Spearmint *(Mentha arvensis)* is the type of mint most often used in Vietnamese cooking, but any type of mint you can find will work nicely. Also called *rau bac ha* and *rau thom,* mint is used often, so try to keep it on hand along with cilantro.

PERILLA *(RAU TIA TO)*

Perilla leaves *(Perilla frutescens)* are large, matte, and beautifully two-toned; deep green on top and rich purple on the underside. *Shiso* is their name in Japan, where they are often used. Sometimes listed on sushi menus as "beefsteak leaves," they make nice little wrappers, in place of *la lot* leaves, for Grilled Leaf-Wrapped Beef Kebabs (page 33), or *bo la lot.*

PIPER LEAF *(LA LOT)*

This beautiful, heart-shaped leaf *(Piper sarmentosum)* is used throughout Southeast Asia as a delicately flavored edible wrapper for savory tidbits. Known in Thailand as *bai cha plu,* it is the namesake ingredient for Grilled Leaf-Wrapped Beef Kebabs (page 33), or *bo la lot.* Piper leaves are not common in the West, but you can use perilla leaves, large basil leaves, spinach leaves, or grape leaves as a wrapper in their place.

RAU RAM

With its bright, pungent flavor and aroma, *rau ram (Polygonum auberti odoratum)* is earning a place for itself among the herbs appreciated in the West. Pale green and smooth, but not shiny, *rau ram* leaves resemble those of Asian basil in overall shape. But unlike basil, a *rau ram* leaf usually sports a dark, handsome mark at its widest point, on both sides of its spine. In Malaysia, Singapore, and Indonesia, it is known as *laksa* leaf because of its role in the pungent seafood noodle soup *laksa.*

RICE PADDY HERB *(RAU NGO OM)*

This little herb sprouts tiny leaves widely spaced over its long, plump little stems. *Rau ngo om (Limnophila aromatica)* is chopped or torn up whole, stems as well as leaves, and then added to soups and curries at serving time. With its petite oval leaves attached to the stem at intervals, from base to tip, *rau ngo om* looks like a sprig of thyme that has been magically inflated. But the resemblance ends there; don't try to replace it with thyme.

SAW-LEAF HERB *(RAU NGO GAI)*

Long, straight, smooth leaves set this aromatic and pungent herb *(Eryngium foetidium)* apart from the crowd. Picture a flat green ribbon as long as your finger and with a delicately serrated edge. Look for *rau ngo gai,* also known in English as saw-tooth herb, on the herb plate whenever you order a bowl of *pho* (page 128).

Rice Noodles and Rice Paper Wrappers

Within the bounty of Asian ingredients widely available to the home cook, none have greater potential for the quick and easy kitchen than dried rice noodles and rice paper wrappers. Many supermarkets stock them nowadays, and so do Asian groceries and mail-order sources (page 162). Their virtues are many: Rice noodles are a foundation for substantial meals at a miniscule cost. They come in many sizes, from wire-thin threads to big, fat, fettuccine-like ribbons. Rice paper wrappers range from small, medium, and large translucent rounds to small triangles, perfect for wrapping up tiny spring rolls. They weigh very little and keep well for ages. Since they are shelf stable, stock up when you come across a supply and keep them on your pantry shelf next to the boxes of spaghetti and macaroni.

Rice noodles offer wonderful options for vegetarians, vegans, and people allergic to wheat. They satisfy, accept flavors beautifully, and cook very fast. Nobody makes better, more creative use of rice noodles and rice paper wrappers than the cooks of Vietnam, so it's time you became better acquainted with them.

Dried Rice Noodles

The major kinds of dried rice noodles differ mostly in their width. You'll find much variation in English-language nomenclature among various packages, but you needn't rely on linguistic markers. Your eyes will tell you all you need to know. For example, the words "rice sticks" and "rice vermicelli" appear on noodles of many different widths. Since you can interchange one width for another in most of these recipes, you can't really go wrong here. Just look through the cellophane wrapping and select the size you want. Here are the three basic sizes in which you will find dried rice noodles:

BANH PHO

These are the linguine-sized noodles used in the signature Vietnamese noodle dish *pho* (page 128). They are also perfect for other soupy noodle dishes, such as *Hu Tieu* Noodles with Pork and Shrimp, Saigon Style (page 131). Thais use *banh pho,* also known as Chantaboon rice noodles, to make their eponymous noodle dish, *paht Thai.*

BUN

These noodles are thin, somewhere between angel hair and spaghetti, but flatter. They might be labeled *"bun,"* but you're more likely to find them called "rice vermicelli" or "rice sticks." Anything thinner than *banh pho* will work just fine. Check out the noodles in a bowl of *bun* at your favorite Vietnamese restaurant, and then hunt for that size. Or better yet, ask the restaurant people if they might show you the noodles they use for their noodle dishes in their uncooked state.

WIDE RICE NOODLES

These will probably be labeled "rice sticks," but even if they aren't, they will look like dried fettuccine: big wide ribbons all folded up in a rectangular bundle. They are my personal favorite, especially for stir-frying.

There are a few other kinds around, but these will get you started. Stay curious and ask for help. Fellow shoppers, grocery store proprietors, waiters, and restaurant owners can be fabulous resources. You never know when it will be your lucky day; culinary advice and wisdom can find you right there in the middle of the grocery aisle.

WORKING WITH NOODLES

For all widths of dried rice noodles, your cook's drill will be the same: soak 'em, drain 'em, and cook 'em. Soaking the noodles is the traditional way to prep them, and it takes only a few minutes. You can soak noodles in advance, drain them well, and then cover, and chill for 1 or 2 days. Using cold soaking water, it takes 20 to 30 minutes. Using warm to hot water speeds the process to 5 to 10 minutes. Softened noodles can be stir-fried or boiled until tender.

Vietnamese Rice Paper Wrappers *(banh trang)*

Brittle round rice paper wrappers and small triangular ones, embossed with a basket-weave design, are the key to *goi cuon* (page 31), or summer rolls, one of the many brilliant culinary inspirations from the kitchens of Vietnam. Think of them as a kind of big, flat, chewy, and salty noodle—one that doesn't even need cooking to be ready to eat. They also enclose crispy *cha gio* spring rolls, and appear alongside salad platters for making wraps at the table.

WORKING WITH RICE PAPER WRAPPERS

Your task is to soften and transfer them from their brittle state, which barely resembles food, into a handy, appealing little wrapper for all kinds of tasty fillings. Some recipes suggest that you brush them with water with a pastry brush, or spritz them with water or beer. I, for one, have gotten nowhere with either of these delicate methods. I prefer a quick soak in a skillet filled with very warm water. My 10-inch skillet is just the right size for one wrapper at a time, and I can easily add hot water from the kettle if the water cools too much before I'm finished rolling. Though many cooks can manage an assembly-line method, I like working with one wrapper at a time. I dunk it and set it out to soften for a minute or two. Then I fill and roll it, set it aside, and start the next one.

More Ingredients for the Vietnamese Kitchen

BEAN THREAD NOODLES *(BUN TAU)*

Also called glass noodles and cellophane noodles, these little wiry skeins are made from mung beans, the same little green pea-sized legume that brings us cool, crunchy bean sprouts. They cook quickly and absorb flavorings beautifully. Vietnamese cooks use them in clear soups, stir-fried dishes (especially those featuring seafood), meat loaf, omelets, and as a major ingredient in the magnificent crisp little spring roll *cha gio*. Asian markets carry *bun tau* in big string bags full of 1- to 2-ounce packages, which are very handy for the pantry shelf. In dried form they look a lot like thin rice noodles, so check the ingredients list for words like "green bean starch," a reference to mung beans in their little green hulls.

BROWN BEAN SAUCE *(TUONG)*

Brown bean sauce is an ancient Asian seasoning of soybeans preserved with salt. It comes in various forms: ground bean sauce, fermented soybeans, bean paste, yellow beans, and yellow bean sauce. They differ a bit in color and texture. Check the ingredients list; you want mostly soybeans and salt. Some versions, including hoisin sauce, have sugar, chilies, and other seasonings. Any of these will work as long as you taste as you go. Avoid Chinese-style black beans, however, as they are too salty and dry to work in place of *tuong*.

CHILI-GARLIC SAUCE *(TUONG OT TOI)*

This thick, red purée of fresh hot chilies makes an outstanding pantry staple. It provides much of what you get by grinding fresh hot chilies in a mortar, and keeps well in the refrigerator. Many grocery stores carry it in plastic jars with a parrot-green lid. The words "*tuong ot toi*" often appear on the label, identifying the product, not a brand name. Though they differ slightly, most other thick hot red chili purées can substitute for chili-garlic sauce. Chinese chili paste is not ideal, as it is made with oil and dried red chilies (not fresh). It will do if you use the chili purée and avoid the oil.

COCONUT MILK, UNSWEETENED *(NUOC DUA)*

Canned coconut milk is really coconut cream, the luxurious essence extracted from the first pressing of grated coconut soaked in water. If you crack open a hairy brown coconut, extract the white, sturdy sweet meat attached to the hard brown shell, grate it finely, soak it in water, and squeeze out several pressings in the standard Southeast Asian way, you will get about four cups of coconut milk, about one-fourth of which will be rich cream. For the purpose of this book, "coconut milk" means the lovely rich liquid stirred well and poured straight from the can. Vietnamese cooks use coconut milk in curries, a few soups, and many sweets and snacks. Canned is great, frozen coconut milk works wonderfully as well, and I've seen cans and packets of dried powder lately that do the job.

DRIED CHINESE MUSHROOMS *(NAM HUONG KHO)*

These are actually dried shiitake mushrooms. They look like they've seen better days, but they revive fast, becoming a delicious, flavor-absorbing vegetable that adds color and texture to soups, noodle dishes, and ground meat dishes such as Vietnamese Meat Loaf (page 75). A 15- to 20-minute immersion in warm water brings them back to their former glory. You'll need to trim away and discard their woody stems. They keep for ages; I transfer them to a jar and have them within easy reach in the pantry.

FISH SAUCE *(NUOC MAM)*

Fish sauce is the quintessential Vietnamese ingredient, used in almost every dish, except sweets. Made from salt-cured anchovies, it provides a rustic flavor and salty, satisfying substance to food. Sometimes it shows its colors proudly, as in Salmon Steaks in Caramel Fish Sauce (page 96). Other times, it harmonizes with other flavors, acting as a subtle source of delicious depth. For people in need of maximum nutrition at minimal expense, fish sauce provides protein and vitamin B. Vietnam is the mother lode for fish sauce aficionados; the island of Phu Quoc is world renowned for the fine quality of its *nuoc mam*. Fish sauce from Thailand is what you will find most often in Asian markets, and it works perfectly in all the recipes in this book.

FIVE-SPICE POWDER *(NGU VI HUONG)*

This fragrant ground seasoning mix is a classic from the Chinese tradition, beloved throughout Asia for the sweet, deep flavor it brings to braised and roasted food, particularly pork, duck, and hard-boiled eggs. Five is a handy number, expressing the presence of an array of aromatic spices rather than an exact count. No matter how many end up in a given version, you can expect that star anise, cinnamon, cloves, and Szechuan peppercorns will be included.

GALANGA *(RIENG)*

This pungent member of the ginger family adds a citrusy tang to Vietnamese dishes, and is often used with fish. Like its first cousins, turmeric, ginger, and *krachai*, *galanga* is thought to provide medicinal value along with its extraordinary aroma and flavor. Fresh *galanga* resembles ginger, but it is rounded and shiny, with thin, dark concentric rings. Frozen *galanga* is widely available, whole or sliced, while dried galanga comes sliced or ground. Frozen and dried *galanga* work well, but the powdered form is merely dust. You can replace *galanga* with fresh ginger in recipes for a different, but harmonious flavor and scent.

GINGER *(GUNG)*

Fresh ginger is a basic ingredient in Vietnamese cooking, beloved for its intense, sweet-and-sharp seasoning powers. It's often cooked with chicken and fish. Fresh ginger can be found in most supermarkets as well as in Asian markets. To chop it, cut off a good chunk, set it, cut side down, on the cutting board, and shave off the peeling. Then cut it crosswise into coins. Stack these up, cut across the stack, making thin strips, and you've got shreds. If you need chopped, go back across the shreds, cutting in the other direction.

GREEN PAPAYA *(DU DU XANH)*

Papaya trees thrive in Vietnam. Their young, green fruit is appreciated as a cool, crunchy salad component, while the luscious, mature, orange-colored flesh is eaten as fruit. Look for ready-to-eat, peeled and shredded fresh green papaya in Asian markets. It makes Green Papaya Salad (page 105) an almost instant dish. To prepare and shred a green papaya, peel half of it lengthwise (the white goo under the green skin is papain, a natural enzyme used in Asia for tenderizing meat). Cut it in half lengthwise, scoop out the seeds, and shred the peeled half on a box grater or in the food processor. Refrigerate the other half for another time. I use shredded cabbage, thinly sliced cucumber, or cooked spaghetti squash strands in place of green papaya when I don't have the real thing.

HOISIN SAUCE *(SOT HOISIN)*

Hoisin is the cousin from the salted preserved soybean family who went to Hollywood and came back a star. Hoisin sauce starts out as *tuong* (see Brown Bean Sauce, page 17), and is seasoned with five-spice powder, garlic, vinegar, sesame oil, and lots of sugar. The result is a thick, intense sauce that is easy to like. Vietnamese cooks use hoisin as a component in dipping sauces, and as a source of deep, rich, sweet flavor and color in marinades and braised dishes.

LEMONGRASS *(XA)*

Fresh lemongrass pervades Vietnamese cooking in a lovely, lyrical way. Used lavishly in marinades, stews, and grilled foods, it provides a warm, tropical breeze entwining cool-climate dishes from the northern region, and refined royal fare from Hue, and the lush, ripe cooking of southern Vietnam. Fresh lemongrass stalks have joined fresh ginger in many supermarkets the past few years, and are standard in Asian markets. If your source is unreliable, buy a supply when you find some and freeze it. Chop off and discard the top half, pull off any dried outer leaves, wrap the bottom tightly, and use it straight from the freezer. It keeps well for several months. Recently, I've found wonderful frozen, finely ground lemongrass imported from Vietnam in clear plastic containers. Don't bother with dried lemongrass and lemongrass powder, as *xa*'s remarkable flavor and aroma fade quickly once it is dried. Most dishes here either don't require lemongrass, or will be almost as tasty without it.

MUNG BEAN CENTERS, YELLOW *(DAU XANH)*

Vietnam loves *dau xanh*—as a source of protein, steamed with both sweet and savory versions of sticky rice, in the parade of sweet coconut milk puddings and drinks enjoyed between meals, and as a component for *banh chung*, the banana leaf–wrapped rice cakes essential to a New Year feast. *Dau* means "bean" and *xanh* means "green," the color of the little yellow bean's hull.

PEANUTS *(DAU PHONG)*

You know what peanuts are, but you may not always have them handy, and you should. Adored especially in the south, they are sprinkled over sticky rice, grilled meats, *Hu Tieu* Noodles with Pork and Shrimp, Saigon Style (page 131), Chicken and Cabbage Salad with Fresh Mint (page 102), and more. I buy a good-sized jar of roasted and salted peanuts, and transfer half the peanuts into two medium-sized jars. One jar is mine for cooking. Since my husband devours peanuts for snacks, he gets his own jar. I store the remaining half in the freezer, since roasted peanuts go stale fast.

SESAME OIL *(HOT ME)*

Made from toasted white sesame seeds (see below), Asian sesame oil is dark brown, a ringer for maple syrup until you catch its divine, nutty aroma and taste its rich, alluring flavor. Vietnamese cooks use *hot me* in sauces, stir-fries, and marinades. I like the Kadoya brand from Japan, which is sold in supermarkets, next to the soy sauce.

SESAME SEEDS, WHITE *(DAU ME)*

Stock up on white sesame seeds; they are a delightful finishing touch to many Vietnamese dishes, from snacks and sweets to grilled food. You can buy them in the spice section of the supermarket, but if you adore them as I do, you may want to buy them at the Asian market in cellophane bags, which are less expensive and will hold you for a while. They can be dry-fried in a hot pan to heighten their flavor, but I like to toast them in the oven, so that they brown evenly without burning. To do this, scatter about ¼ cup white sesame seeds in a pie pan and place it in a 400°F oven for 10 to 12 minutes, until the sesame seeds are nicely browned. Turn them out onto a plate to cool completely, transfer to a jar, and keep at room temperature for up to 1 month. Toasted sesame seeds chopped with peanuts and then mixed with sugar make a spectacularly delicious traditional topping for Sticky Rice (page 117).

TAMARIND AND TAMARIND LIQUID *(ME; NUOC ME CHUA)*

Tamarind fruit dangles from huge hardwood trees throughout Southeast Asia in big, fat, C-shaped pods. They ripen to a rich, soft, dark pulp, filled with seeds and enclosed in a brittle, light brown shell. Tamarind liquid is made by soaking ripe tamarind pulp and pressing it through a strainer to create a thick, luscious purée that is earthy brown, smoky, sour, and sweet. You can buy blocks of tamarind pulp, processed enough to remove most of the seeds and stringy stuff between you and the lovely smoky-sweet-sour flavor it provides. You still need to soak, mash, and strain out the essence, a messy bit of work for a quick and easy cook. To make tamarind liquid, put about ½ cup of tamarind pulp in a bowl with 1 cup of warm water. Soak for 15 to 20 minutes, pressing and mashing now and then to soften the pulp and mix it with the water. Strain through a fine-mesh strainer into another bowl, pressing and scraping with a large spoon to extract as much liquid and purée as you can. You will have about ¾ cup. I am happy with ready-to-use tamarind liquid imported from Thailand. It looks a lot like apple butter, dark and thick, and it is delicious. It's called "concentrate cooking tamarind" on one good brand, Garden Queen (tall plastic jar, bright blue lid). You'll also see the Vietnamese words for tamarind liquid, *nuoc me chua,* on the label. In a pinch, I also use Indian-style tamarind chutney in place of tamarind liquid, with tasty results.

TURMERIC *(BOT NGHE)*

This knobby cousin of ginger and *galanga* is beloved not for its flavor (quite mild, even when it is fresh), but for its outrageous, gloriously gaudy yellow-orange hue, which it transmits to food and everything else it touches. The source of curry powder's trademark color, turmeric has been prized for centuries as a dye for cloth, including the traditional robes of Theravada Buddhist monks. Whole rhizomes of turmeric can sometimes be found fresh or frozen in Asian markets nowadays, but ground turmeric powder works fine in these recipes. It's widely used in Vietnam, transmitting its gorgeous golden color to such dishes as *Cha Ca* Fish with Fresh Dill, Hanoi Style (page 89).

USEFUL UTENSILS FOR COOKING VIETNAMESE FOOD

BIG NOODLE BOWLS AND TINY SAUCERS

While you are in an Asian market stocking up on ingredients, check out the housewares shelves. Usually you will find an array of porcelain and plastic serving pieces, large and small. To enjoy and appreciate Vietnamese dishes, especially the fabulous noodle creations and numerous sprightly dipping sauces, you will need a few new dishes: Consider buying the big, deep, and wide bowls designed for individual servings of noodles in broth, as in *Pho* Noodles with Beef, Hanoi Style (page 128), or dry noodles with a dressing, as in Big, Cool Noodle Bowl with Roast Chicken, Cucumbers, and Fresh Mint (page 133). Get at least four; cooking this food magically conjures up guests.

Get a good supply of the tiny saucers and small shallow bowls designed to hold individual portions of dipping sauces and condiments. These are also useful for holding prepped ingredients to be placed by the stove for a stir-fry.

KNIVES

Good knives will serve you well, especially when you cook Vietnamese food. Ideally, you should have a well-made paring knife and either a big Chinese cleaver or a 10-inch chef's knife. You will find sturdy, all-metal cleavers from China in many Asian markets.

CUTTING BOARD

You also need a good, sturdy cutting board; several if you have the storage space. I like to keep one for meat and fish and two for vegetables, fruits, and herbs, to avoid cross-contamination between raw meats and other foods. To keep your cutting board from sliding around the counter as you chop, wet a clean kitchen towel, squeeze it out well, and place it on the countertop. Put your cutting board on the towel, and it should stay put.

TONGS, SPATULAS, AND BIG SPOONS FOR STIR-FRYING

Treat yourself to a double set of big, V-shaped, spring-mounted stainless steel tongs, one long, and the other extra long. They come in handy for cooking noodles, so important in Vietnamese cuisine, and also help with stir-frying, grilling, and more. Have a sturdy metal or heat-resistant plastic spatula and a slotted spoon available, too, for stove-top cooking. The spatula helps you turn over large quantities of food quickly, and the slotted spoon lets you scoop food away from the heat when you need to act fast.

POTS AND PANS

In Vietnam, the wok is a basic kitchen tool. Woks are wonderful, and even a good electric wok works well for most dishes. Though it takes up counter space, it frees your stove for simmering pots, and the solid, balanced base keeps it steady while you scoop and stir. While I love my big, heavy, carbon-steel wok, I actually do most of my cooking in a large, deep, black cast-iron skillet. It heats up fast, holds heat well, handles large quantities of food, and is designed for a flat-top, Western-style stove like mine. Any large, deep skillet will serve you well, along with a small skillet and a few saucepans. A big Dutch oven with a tight-fitting lid is great for curry, and can serve as the base for an improvised steamer.

ELECTRIC RICE COOKER

Rice is at the heart of Vietnamese cuisine, and an electric rice cooker simplifies the task of cooking it. You measure the rice into the pot, rinse, swish, and drain it well. Then add the proper amount of water, easily measured on the side of the pot. Press a button, and you are free. Mix up a batch of Everyday Dipping Sauce (page 156), put away groceries, or call your beloved sister in Seattle and chat. When you hear that delicate ping, you know that perfectly delicious rice awaits you. I suggest a big rice cooker, 5 to 10 cups, since it is versatile enough to make a mere 2 to 3 cups as well as a great big batch when guests are expected. I like to cook extra rice because it reheats so nicely and can easily become fried rice (page 122).

DEVICES FOR STEAMING FOOD

In most Asian kitchens, steaming is a basic, everyday cooking process. Asian markets and mail-order sources (page 162) often carry traditional steaming equipment. For steaming Sticky Rice (page 117), look for a Laotian-style two-piece steamer, a simple cone-shaped woven basket and a deep, lightweight pot. The basket, which holds the soaked and drained sticky rice, fits into the pot, suspending the rice over several inches of steaming water. The steamer is perfect for the job, widely available, and cheap. For steaming a variety of foods, including sticky rice, look for big Chinese-style, lightweight metal steamers, consisting of a stack of perforated trays fitted over a wide base. The food to be steamed is placed on banana leaves lining the trays, or in bowls or on plates set on the trays. In addition to these two complete steamer sets, you can find both simple wire racks and handsome stacked sets of bamboo trays, both of which fit into a wok, resting snugly over several inches of steaming water. For bamboo tray sets, bigger is better since a wider tray can hold more food per steaming session.

You can also improvise a steamer. Use a pasta pot with an insert, or a stockpot or big Dutch oven and an empty tuna can, converted into a steaming ring. For the pasta pot, bring several inches of water to a boil in the pot, place a shallow heat-proof bowl or plate of food in the perforated insert, and lower the insert into the pot for steaming. For the stockpot or Dutch oven, remove the bottom lid and the label from an empty tuna can, leaving a wide ring. Place this steaming ring on the bottom of the pot and add water to a depth of about 3 inches. Put the food you are steaming on a heat-proof plate, pie pan, or shallow bowl and balance it on the ring. Bring the water to a boil, cover, and steam until the food is cooked.

BLENDER, MINI–FOOD PROCESSOR, AND MORTAR AND PESTLE

For turning fresh lemongrass, garlic, shallots, and herbs into flavorful marinades and sauces, you can use a blender or a small-capacity food processor. You will usually need to pause and scrape down the sides during the process. You may also need to add water to get the blades moving so that everything is ground together smoothly and well.

If you would prefer to use a traditional heavy mortar and pestle, called *vua* or *ho,* look among the cookware in an Asian grocery store (check the bottom shelf first). The squat, bluish black mortar and its pestle are made entirely of granite. Ranging in size from tiny to huge, this ancient "food processor of Asia" pulverizes lemongrass, ginger, and other tough customers with a little upper arm action and a little time. You can also use a mortar and pestle to grind up toasted sesame seeds, peanuts, and toasted rice grains for Vietnamese dishes. Of course a mortar and pestle are useful for Western food, too. They can make fabulous pesto, smash toffee to put on ice cream, or grind a supply of black or white peppercorns. They are beautiful, and you'll think of more uses once you have them.

Pho *Noodles with Beef, Hanoi Style; page 128*

APPETIZERS & SNACKS

The playful nature of Vietnamese cooking is nowhere more evident than in the skewered, bundled, wrapped, or rolled foods that make up this chapter. From ethereal summer rolls to the most spectacularly delicious submarine sandwich on planet Earth, these recipes allow you to turn out lots of flavor in a small amount of time.

Lemongrass Shrimp (page 26) put Vietnam's official herbal ambassador on full display, and the simple marinade is equally tasty on fish. Sugarcane Shrimp (page 27) delight the eye and come together fast because they are made with canned sugarcane.

Many of these goodies are cooked on the grill, but don't despair if that won't work for you. Use a grill pan, countertop grilling machine, broiler, skillet, or even a hot oven. However you cook them, you will find they are ready fast and disappear even faster from the plates of delighted friends and family members.

MAKES ABOUT 30 SMALL SKEWERS

LEMONGRASS SHRIMP

tom nuong xa

This inviting starter requires only a little chopping, measuring, and processing for the marinade, and a quick turn on the grill. The resulting dish looks and tastes delicious. If you prefer to cook the shrimp indoors, simply broil them in a very hot oven, or sear them in a pan, and then stick them on skewers once they're cooked to make serving easier. You could even roast them in a 425°F oven for 3 to 5 minutes—they may not be golden brown, but they'll be gorgeously pink and completely delicious. Consider leaving the tails on as you peel the shrimp. The tail turns a bright red during the cooking, providing a flash of beautiful color to delight your eyes, and a little handle for eating these treats.

3 tablespoons coarsely chopped fresh lemongrass

1 tablespoon chopped garlic

2 tablespoons fish sauce

2 tablespoons freshly squeezed lime juice

1 tablespoon soy sauce

1 tablespoon vegetable oil

1 tablespoon Caramel Sauce (page 158) **or brown sugar**

1 tablespoon sugar

½ teaspoon salt

1 pound medium shrimp, peeled and deveined

About 30 small bamboo skewers, soaked in water for at least 30 minutes

In a blender or mini–food processor, combine the lemongrass, garlic, fish sauce, lime juice, soy sauce, oil, Caramel Sauce, sugar, and salt. Blend until fairly smooth, pulsing on and off and scraping down the sides to keep the texture uniform. Add 1 or 2 tablespoons of water, as needed, to move the blades. Transfer the marinade to a medium bowl, add the shrimp, and toss to coat well. Set aside for 20 to 30 minutes.

Build a hot charcoal fire, preheat a gas grill or the broiler, preheat the oven to 425°F, or lightly oil a skillet or grill pan and heat until very hot. Thread the shrimp onto skewers, 2 or 3 per skewer, and cook on the hot grill, turning once, until the shrimp are pink and cooked through, 2 to 4 minutes. Or place in a lightly greased pan and cook under the broiler for 2 to 4 minutes, or roast in the oven for 3 to 5 minutes. Or sauté quickly in the skillet or grill pan for 2 to 4 minutes. Serve the shrimp hot, warm, or at room temperature.

SUGARCANE SHRIMP

chao tom

Sugarcane is available in cans, peeled and trimmed and ready to eat, so you can easily make this signature Vietnamese presentation at home. A simple, lightly seasoned shrimp mixture is pressed onto a rod of sugarcane and grilled just until firm and pink. Traditionally, the shrimp are minced, seasoned with roasted rice powder, enriched with a little pork fat, and then ground to a smooth paste. This makes for a firm, chewy texture. My version is coarsely ground so that the shrimp mixture is easier to work with, and it is still delicious.

Chao tom are often steamed and then grilled, but cooking them without that initial step works fine. Grilling is the ticket to those handsome grill marks, but I've made this sensational treat in a grill pan, in a skillet on top of the stove, under a broiler, and in a hot oven. However you cook them, your *chao tom* will look and taste delicious. If the lack of sugarcane is keeping you from trying this brilliant dish, shape the shrimp mixture into small patties and fry them in a hot, well-oiled skillet.

1 pound medium shrimp, peeled, deveined, and coarsely chopped

1 egg white, lightly beaten

2 tablespoons coarsely chopped green onion

1 tablespoon finely chopped garlic

1 tablespoon vegetable oil

1 tablespoon fish sauce

½ teaspoon sugar

½ teaspoon salt

½ teaspoon black pepper

4 peeled sugarcane stalks, each about 6 inches long (half of a 48-ounce can)

Everyday Dipping Sauce (page 156)

20 Boston, Bibb, or other lettuce leaves (optional)

1 cup fresh cilantro, mint, or basil leaves, or a mix (optional)

In a medium bowl, combine the shrimp with the egg white, green onion, garlic, oil, fish sauce, sugar, salt, and pepper. Stir to mix everything well.

Transfer to a food processor and pulse briefly, 3 to 5 times, just enough to blend all ingredients together into a very rough paste, with little chunks of shrimp still visible. Or blend in a blender, stopping to scrape down the sides. Or use a knife to mince the shrimp by hand. Return the shrimp mixture to the bowl. If you have time, cover and refrigerate for 30 minutes or so; this makes the mixture a bit easier to handle.

Set out the sugarcane stalks on a work surface, and have the shrimp mixture and a small bowl of water at hand. Cut each stalk of sugarcane in half crosswise, to make 8 short stalks. Then cut each short stalk lengthwise into quarters, to make a total of 32 stalks, about 3 inches long.

■ *continued*

Dip your hands in water, and put 1 tablespoon of the shrimp mixture in the palm of your left hand. Press a 3-inch sugarcane skewer into the shrimp mixture, and then mold the shrimp mixture to encircle the skewer. Press to seal the shrimp to the cane, leaving both ends free to use as handles. Set aside on a plate while you prepare the remaining skewers in the same fashion.

Build a hot charcoal fire, preheat a gas grill or the broiler, preheat the oven to 400°F, or lightly oil a grill pan or skillet until very hot. Place the sugarcane shrimp on the lightly oiled surface of the grill rack and cook, turning often, until the shrimp are pink, nicely browned on the outside, cooked to the center, and firm to the touch, 2 to 4 minutes. Or cook under the broiler, or in the oven for 5 to 7 minutes, or in the hot skillet or grill pan, turning often, until browned and cooked through.

Transfer the shrimp to a serving platter and serve hot or warm, with Everyday Dipping Sauce. If using lettuce and herbs, make little packets by tucking a chunk of shrimp and a few fresh herb leaves into a lettuce leaf and rolling it up. Dip this bundle into the sauce as you eat.

SUMMER ROLLS WITH SHRIMP AND MINT

goi cuon

Goi cuon are known in English as "summer rolls," "rice paper rolls," "soft spring rolls," and "salad rolls," the latter a direct translation of their Vietnamese name. These extraordinary rice paper–wrapped bundles of shrimp, rice noodles, lettuce, and fresh mint present an edible sketch of Vietnamese cuisine. Delicate and satisfying, soft and crunchy, as plain as white rice noodles and yet vibrant with the pink and green of shrimp and fresh mint, these snacks invite you to savor the contrasting pleasures of Vietnam's way with food. Get a little assembly line going with a friend or two, and you will quickly wrap and roll enough *goi cuon* for your picnic or party. Serve them with Everyday Dipping Sauce (page 156), bottled peanut sauce, or a small bowl of hoisin sauce topped with chopped peanuts and a dollop of chili-garlic sauce.

½ pound thin dried rice noodles, angel hair pasta, or somen noodles

12 round rice paper sheets, about 8 inches in diameter

10 Bibb, Boston, or other tender lettuce leaves, cut crosswise into 1-inch strips (about 2 cups loosely packed)

½ cup fresh mint leaves

½ cup fresh cilantro leaves

5 green onions, trimmed, cut into 3-inch lengths, and then cut lengthwise into thin strips

12 medium shrimp, cooked, peeled, and halved lengthwise

Dipping sauce of your choice for serving

Bring a medium saucepan of water to a rolling boil over high heat. Drop in the rice noodles, and remove from the heat. Let stand 8 to 10 minutes, gently lifting and stirring the noodles now and then as they soften to keep them separate and to cook them evenly. Drain, rinse with cold water, drain well, and set aside. You should have about 2 cups of noodles.

Arrange all the ingredients in separate dishes around a large cutting board or tray set before you. Have a large platter ready to hold the finished rolls, and fill a large skillet or shallow bowl with hot water.

■ *continued*

To make each roll, slide 1 sheet of rice paper into the pan of water and press gently to submerge it for about 15 seconds. Remove it carefully, draining the water, and place it before you on the cutting board.

On the bottom third of the sheet, line up the following ingredients in a horizontal row: a small tangle of noodles (about ¼ cup), some lettuce strips, some mint leaves, and some cilantro leaves. Sprinkle green onion slivers on top.

Lift the wrapper edge nearest to you and roll it up and over the filling, tucking it in under them about halfway along the wrapper and compressing everything gently into a cylindrical shape. When you've completely enclosed the filling in one good turn, fold in the sides tightly, as though making an envelope. Then place 2 shrimp halves, pink side down, on the rice sheet just above the cylinder. Continue rolling up the wrapper and press the seam to close it, wetting it with a little splash of water if it has dried out too much to seal itself closed. Set the roll aside on the platter to dry, seam side down. Continue to fill and roll up the rice paper sheets until you have made 8 to 10 rolls. Set aside.

To serve, present the rolls whole, or cut them in half crosswise—straight or on the diagonal. Or trim away the ends and cut into bite-sized lengths.

GRILLED LEAF-WRAPPED BEEF KEBABS *bo la lot*

Handsome and delicious, these plump little cylinders of lemongrass-infused beef are one of the dishes featured in the classic northern-style feast, *bo bay mon,* or "seven-course beef." The standard wrapper is the *la lot* leaf (also known as piper leaf or pepper leaf), a lovely and delicate heart-shaped edible leaf enjoyed throughout Southeast Asia. Since *la lot* leaves are a rare find in the West, I make the kebabs with preserved grape leaves from a Middle Eastern market, which I rinse and stem. You can also use big flat spinach leaves, or large leaves of fresh basil laid side by side, or the herb perilla, also known by its Japanese name, *shiso*. Roll them up as you would stuffed grape leaves, but leaving the ends exposed.

½ pound ground beef

2 tablespoons minced freshed lemongrass

1 tablespoon finely chopped shallots or onion

1 tablespoon finely chopped garlic

1 tablespoon fish sauce

1 tablespoon vegetable oil

1 teaspoon sugar

1 teaspoon black pepper

½ teaspoon salt

½ teaspoon ground turmeric (optional)

30 to 40 *la lot*, grape, flat spinach, large basil, or perilla leaves

About 10 long bamboo skewers, soaked in water for at least 30 minutes

Everyday Dipping Sauce (page 156)

■ *continued*

In a medium bowl, combine the ground beef with the lemongrass, shallots, garlic, fish sauce, oil, sugar, pepper, salt, and turmeric, if using, and mix well. Divide the mixture into generous tablespoons of meat, and shape each portion into a plump little cylinder about 2 inches long. If you are using Mediterranean-style grape leaves, rinse well and trim away any stems.

Place a leaf on a cutting board with the veined side down and the stem end toward you, and place a meat portion at the edge nearest you. Roll it up in the leaf and place it, seam side down, on a platter. Leave the ends open, unless you are using grape leaves, which need their sides tucked in because they are wide. Continue rolling in this way until all the meat is wrapped in leaves.

Build a hot charcoal fire, preheat a gas grill, or preheat the oven to 400°F. To grill the kebabs, thread 3 or 4 rolls onto each skewer, bunching them up near the pointed end, and taking care to pierce each roll through the seam. Place the skewers on the oiled rack of the hot grill and cook until done, 2 to 3 minutes per side, turning once or twice. To bake them, place the rolls (without skewers), seam side down, in a 13-x-9-inch pan and bake until done, 8 to 10 minutes. Transfer to a serving platter and serve hot, warm, or at room temperature with dipping sauce.

MAKES ABOUT 3 DOZEN MEATBALLS

PORK MEATBALLS WITH FRESH HERBS AND RICE NOODLES IN LETTUCE CUPS

nem nuong

These tasty little meatballs star in a classic roll-up of rice noodles and fresh herbs in lettuce cups. A specialty of the town of Nha Trang in central Vietnam, they are enjoyed throughout the country. Traditionally *nem nuong* are made with pork that is sliced and then ground to a very smooth paste. I use already ground pork, which is simpler and yields a pleasing, meaty texture. Invite your guests to wrap a meatball or two in a lettuce cup along with some rice noodles, scallions, and fresh herbs, and then dip the package into either the Hoisin-Peanut or Everyday Dipping Sauce. Or serve the meatballs with a dipping sauce as part of a barbecued feast.

FOR THE MEATBALLS

1 pound ground pork

1 tablespoon vegetable oil

1 tablespoon finely chopped shallots or onion

1 tablespoon finely chopped garlic

2 tablespoons fish sauce

1 tablespoon soy sauce

1 teaspoon sugar

½ teaspoon salt

½ teaspoon black pepper

ACCOMPANIMENTS

½ pound thin dried rice noodles, softened in warm water for at least 15 minutes

About 36 small, cup-shaped lettuce leaves, preferably Boston, Bibb, or iceberg

1½ cups fresh cilantro, mint, or basil sprigs, or a mix of all three

1 cup thinly sliced green onion or garlic chives cut into 1-inch lengths

Hoisin-Peanut Dipping Sauce (page 159)

Double recipe Everyday Dipping Sauce (page 156; about 1 cup)

12 to 15 bamboo skewers, soaked in water for at least 30 minutes

To begin the meatballs, combine all the ingredients in a medium bowl and mix well with your hands or a big spoon. (For a classic finely ground version, transfer the meat mixture to a food processor and process for 2 to 3 minutes, stopping once or twice to scrape down the bowl, until you have a fairly smooth paste.) Cover and chill for a few minutes while you prepare the accompaniments.

To cook the soaked rice noodles, drain them, drop them into boiling water, and immediately remove from the heat. Let stand 10 minutes, and then drain well. Pile the noodles on a large serving platter, and place the lettuce leaves beside them. Put the herbs and green onion in small bowls and arrange on the platter as well. Place bowls of Hoisin-Peanut Sauce and Everyday Dipping Sauce in the center of the platter, leaving room for the meatballs.

Shape the meat mixture into meatballs, using about 1 tablespoon each for large, walnut-sized meatballs, and about half that amount for the classic *nem nuong.* (Use a little vegetable oil on your palms or spoon if needed to help you shape the meatballs.)

If grilling, build a hot charcoal fire or preheat a gas grill. Thread 3 to 5 meatballs on each skewer, and place them on a plate. Cook on the hot grill, turning now and then, until nicely browned and cooked through, 10 to 15 minutes. To pan-fry the meatballs, heat 1 tablespoon of vegetable oil in a large skillet over medium-high heat. When the pan is hot, add the meatballs and cook, shaking the pan now and then to brown them evenly and cook through, 3 to 5 minutes. Remove from the heat, and thread on skewers if you like, 3 or 4 per skewer. Transfer the grilled or pan-fried meatballs to the prepared serving platter and serve hot or warm. Make little packets by tucking a meatball, a small tangle of noodles, and a pinch of herb leaves and green onion into a lettuce leaf and rolling it up. Dip this bundle into the sauce as you eat.

MAKES 4 SANDWICHES

SUBMARINE SANDWICHES, SAIGON STYLE

banh mi

Welcome to the easiest recipe in the book, accessible to anyone in possession of its fairly common fixin's: good bread; a slice or two of something substantial like ham, roast pork, grilled vegetables, or hard-boiled eggs; cucumber slices; mayonnaise or butter, or both; and the three secret ingredients elevating this pedestrian sandwich to celestial, Vietnamese-inspired heights. Said ingredients are whole leafy sprigs of fresh cilantro; thin, diagonally sliced ovals of fresh jalapeño chilies; and a generous dose of Everyday Pickled Carrots.

You can also indulge your own wishes here. Include traditional Vietnamese cold cuts such as *cha lua* or *cha que*. Add untraditional items like lettuce and tomato, avocado, or alfalfa sprouts. Or cut the sandwich into 3-inch sections and serve it on silver trays as dynamite canapés. What you cannot do is omit the secret ingredients, which I discovered by opening up my first *banh mi* many years ago, in search of the mysterious essence that made a simple and familiar sandwich taste so extraordinarily good. All I found making this magic were cilantro, chilies, and pickled carrots. I wouldn't omit the chilies. Even chiliphobes should try the real thing because the effect is subtle rather than intense. But without the chilies, it's still wonderful. The closer you can come to a warm, freshly baked baguette, the better. Fabulous market versions of *banh mi* sold all over the Mekong Delta are made with bread that is fresh but no longer warm, however, and they are still divine. When I can, I use partially baked and then frozen demi-baguettes from the grocery store. Even without these, you will love *banh mi* and feel like a culinary genius every time you serve them.

4 small baguettes, or 2 regular baguettes cut into four 6-inch sections

Mayonnaise or butter at room temperature, or some of each, for spreading

Prepared soft and spreadable French-style pâté (optional; available in small cans in Asian markets and gourmet shops)

12 slices of cold cuts: Vietnamese pâtés such as *cha lua* or *cha que*, thinly sliced ham or turkey, or Chinese barbecue *(char siu)*

1 hothouse cucumber or 3 small pickling cucumbers, peeled and cut lengthwise into ¼-inch-thick strips

1 cup Everyday Pickled Carrots (page 108)

4 fresh jalapeño chilies, cut diagonally into thin ovals, or 1 tablespoon chili-garlic sauce or any hot sauce

About 24 sprigs fresh cilantro

Slice halfway into the side of each small baguette or section of a large one, leaving one long side attached. Set up a little assembly line, placing the 4 little loaves on a cutting board, handy to all the ingredients and condiments.

Generously spread both sides of each loaf with mayonnaise or butter, or both. Spread a nice dollop of pâté (if using) thinly over the top half of each sandwich.

Place 3 slices of cold cuts on the bottom half of each sandwich, and top with cucumber strips. Divide the pickled carrots among the 4 sandwiches, spreading out the carrots over the meat and cucumber, and adding a spoonful of the brine to each serving. Lay several jalapeño slices along each row of fillings, and top with 6 cilantro sprigs.

Close each sandwich, press gently to bring the flavors together, and serve at room temperature. Or wrap each sandwich tightly in waxed paper, plastic wrap, or foil, and set aside until serving time.

SOUPS

Soup in Vietnam can be deliciously assertive or demure, a hearty centerpiece dish or a simple complement to a big, rice-centered meal. These soups range from simple to fancy, though none requires a great deal of time or work.

Start with Meatball Soup (page 42), wonderful, fast, and satisfying, or the lovely and delicate Clear Soup with Catfish, Tomatoes, and Fresh Dill (page 45). Either of these would work nicely served over rice or noodles as a meal in a bowl.

Pork and Cabbage Rolls in Clear Soup (page 46) is comfort food dressed up with a handsome presentation for nights when you have a little extra time. In case you hunger for it on a busy night, I also give you a shortcut. Sweet and Tangy Soup with Pineapple, Tamarind, and Shrimp (page 48) is a hearty, classic Vietnamese soup open to substitutions: use salmon instead of shrimp, or make it a seafood showboat with clams, scallops, shrimp, and chunks of fish. Shrimp Dumpling Soup with Watercress (page 44) takes a little time to put together, but what a reward—a green and pink creation that is peppery and good. Crab and Asparagus Soup (page 50) is elegant but still easy, and a beauty with fresh asparagus turned a bright green. Vietnamese people have soup at almost every meal, and with these dishes in your repertoire, you may want to follow suit.

SERVES 4 TO 6

MEATBALL SOUP

bo vien

Make this anytime you crave the comfort of hearty homemade soup in a hurry. In the classic version of *bo vien,* cooks grind the beef to a fine paste, creating a firm meatball with the chewy texture beloved throughout Asia. My streamlined version made with ground beef puts this dish on your table in a flash. If you add a fistful or two of tender spinach leaves to the soup, it's a meal. Enjoy this Vietnamese style, along with rice and other dishes. Or savor it as we often do, ladled over noodles or rice in a big soup bowl for a one-dish supper accompanied by chili-garlic sauce or crusty bread.

FOR THE MEATBALLS

1 pound ground beef

2 tablespoons fish sauce

2 tablespoons soy sauce

1 teaspoon Asian sesame oil

1 teaspoon cornstarch

1 teaspoon salt

¼ teaspoon black pepper

FOR THE SOUP

4 cups chicken broth or water

1 tablespoon fish sauce

1 tablespoon soy sauce

1 teaspoon Asian sesame oil

¼ teaspoon black pepper

2 tablespoons thinly sliced green onion

2 tablespoons coarsely chopped fresh cilantro

To make the meatballs, combine the ground beef with all its seasonings in a medium bowl and mix to blend well. Shape into meatballs, using about 1 tablespoon of the mixture for each one. You should have 25 to 30 meatballs.

To make the soup, bring the broth to a rolling boil in a medium saucepan over high heat. Drop in half the meatballs, and cook, stirring now and then, until cooked through, 3 to 5 minutes. Transfer to a bowl with a slotted spoon, cook the remaining meatballs in the broth, and transfer them to the bowl as well.

Season the broth in the saucepan by stirring in the fish sauce, soy sauce, sesame oil, and pepper. Return the meatballs to the broth and heat through. Sprinkle with the green onion and cilantro. Serve hot.

SERVES 4

SHRIMP DUMPLING SOUP WITH WATERCRESS

canh tom

In Vietnam, you'll find this terrific soup made with either finely ground shrimp shaped into springy little quenelles or whole shrimp, marinated in seasonings. I like an in-between version, with the shrimp coarsely ground to a chunky texture so the soup is pleasing to eat and ready fast. I often use fresh spinach leaves or shredded napa cabbage in place of the watercress, which is sometimes difficult to find. If you want to spend a little extra time, seal the shrimp mixture into wonton wrappers and cook them in boiling water until the noodle wrapper and shrimp are cooked. Then place them in a serving bowl, add hot soup with greens, and serve at once.

FOR THE SHRIMP DUMPLINGS

¼ pound medium shrimp, peeled and deveined

1 tablespoon minced green onion

1 teaspoon fish sauce

¼ teaspoon salt

¼ teaspoon black pepper

FOR THE SOUP

3 cups chicken broth

1 cup water

1 tablespoon fish sauce

¼ teaspoon salt

1 ½ cups coarsely chopped watercress or spinach leaves, or finely shredded napa cabbage

To make the dumplings, coarsely chop each shrimp into 3 or 4 pieces and put in a medium bowl. Add the green onion, fish sauce, salt, and pepper and mix well. Transfer to the bowl of a mini–food processor and grind to a very coarse paste, alternately pulsing and checking the mixture to make sure the texture remains coarse—more lumpy than pasty. Transfer to a small bowl and let stand 10 to 15 minutes. (To prepare by hand, chop the shrimp as finely as you can and add to the bowl. Or leave the shrimp whole and combine with the seasonings in a bowl, using your hands to blend well.)

To prepare the soup, bring the broth, water, fish sauce, and salt to a rolling boil in a medium saucepan over medium-high heat. Reduce the heat to maintain the liquid at a gentle boil. Scoop up a tablespoon of the shrimp mixture and drop it gently into the soup, using another spoon to coax it along as needed. Continue scooping up and adding dumplings until you've used up the shrimp mixture, and then cook for about 3 minutes more. Add the watercress, stir well, and remove from the heat. Serve at once.

SERVES 4

CLEAR SOUP WITH CATFISH, TOMATOES, AND FRESH DILL

ca nau ngot

Cooks in Vietnam and neighboring Laos often season fish dishes with fresh dill. You will love its delicate flavor in this speedy soup, which works fine with shrimp as well as fish. If fresh dill is difficult to find, use fresh cilantro or basil, or 2 tablespoons of dried dill, and add a squeeze of lime juice to the serving bowl just before you eat.

4 cups chicken broth or water

¾ pound catfish fillets, or tilapia, salmon, or other firm-fleshed fish

5 plum tomatoes, cored

1 tablespoon fish sauce

½ teaspoon salt

¼ teaspoon black pepper

2 tablespoons thinly sliced green onion

¼ cup coarsely chopped fresh dill

Bring the broth to a rolling boil in a medium saucepan over high heat. Meanwhile, cut the fish into generous chunks. Cut the tomatoes into chunks as well.

Add the fish to the saucepan, lower the heat, and cook the fish in the gently boiling broth until done, 1 to 2 minutes. Stir in the tomatoes, fish sauce, salt, pepper, green onion, and dill, and then quickly remove the soup from the heat. Serve hot.

SERVES 4 TO 6

PORK AND CABBAGE ROLLS IN CLEAR SOUP

canh cai bap nhoi thit

These plump little cabbage bundles of savory pork look delicious in the clear broth, and although they take a little time, the results are worth it. For a quicker version, shape the seasoned pork mixture into 16 to 18 small meatballs. Drop them into the boiling soup, simmer until they're cooked, and add 2 cups of shredded cabbage, chopped bok choy, or fresh spinach leaves. Cook for a minute or two until the cabbage or spinach leaves are vivid green and tender, and serve hot. Thinly slice the green onions and sprinkle them over the finished soup along with the cilantro.

FOR THE SOUP

5 cups chicken broth

2 tablespoons fish sauce

½ teaspoon sugar

½ teaspoon salt

FOR THE CABBAGE ROLLS

8 to 10 large, or 20 small, cabbage leaves

6 to 8 green onions, trimmed, white part coarsely chopped, and green part left whole

½ pound ground pork

1 tablespoon fish sauce

1 teaspoon Asian sesame oil

½ teaspoon sugar

½ teaspoon salt

½ teaspoon black pepper

2 tablespoons coarsely chopped fresh cilantro

To make the soup, in a medium saucepan, bring the broth, fish sauce, sugar, and salt to a rolling boil over medium-high heat and adjust the heat to maintain a gentle boil.

Meanwhile, begin the cabbage rolls: Make a small, V-shaped cut into the base of each cabbage leaf, removing most of the thick rib. Cut the larger leaves in half lengthwise, and place all the leaves on a platter by the stove, along with the green onion tops and a pair of tongs or 2 forks for handling the vegetables as you soften them in the soup.

Submerge one or several cabbage leaves in the hot soup just until they are wilted and pliable but not cooked, about 1 minute. Transfer to the platter, and cook remaining leaves, and then set aside. Plunge the green onion tops down into the soup as well, count to 10, and transfer them to the platter. Remove the soup from the heat and set aside. Rinse the cabbage leaves and green onion tops in cool water, drain, and blot dry. Set aside near a cutting board.

To make the filling for the cabbage rolls, combine the pork, fish sauce, sesame oil, sugar, salt, and pepper in a medium bowl, add the chopped green onion (the white part), and mix well. To prepare the cabbage rolls, place a cabbage leaf on your cutting board with the stem end closest to you and the veiny side down. Place a generous tablespoon of filling near the stem and shape it into a little cylinder. Fold in the sides and roll up from stem to stern, enclosing the meat in a little parcel. Place it on the platter, seam side down, and roll up the rest of the meat in the same fashion. Tear the softened green onion tops in half lengthwise, and tie one strip around each bundle, making a small knot on top, to hold the cabbage wrapper in place. (You can tuck loose ends under, trim them, or leave them free.)

When all the cabbage rolls are made, return the soup to a rolling boil, and then adjust the heat to maintain an active simmer. Carefully lower each cabbage roll into the soup on a spoon. Take your time in order to keep them intact and yourself unsplashed. Cook just until the meat is done, 5 to 7 minutes. Transfer the rolls to a serving bowl or individual soup bowls, ladle the hot soup on top, and sprinkle with the cilantro. Serve hot.

SERVES 6 TO 8

SWEET AND TANGY SOUP WITH PINEAPPLE, TAMARIND, AND SHRIMP

canh chua tom

This classic soup captures Vietnam's cuisine in one delicious bowl: fresh seafood from her endless coastline; tangy tamarind from sturdy trees; luscious pineapples from the fields; garlic, tomatoes, and lemongrass from the garden. This bounty comes together in a glorious soup, often savored in tandem with *ca kho to,* catfish simmered in a clay pot in a sweet and salty caramel sauce. The ingredients list for this soup is a bit long, but everything comes together fast. With rice and a simple salad, you've got a wonderful meal. For *canh chua ca,* make this memorable soup with big chunks of catfish or other firm-fleshed fish.

2 stalks fresh lemongrass

1 tablespoon vegetable oil

1 tablespoon finely chopped garlic

5 cups chicken broth or water

¼ cup prepared tamarind liquid, Indian-style tamarind chutney, or 3 tablespoons vinegar mixed with 1 tablespoon brown sugar

2 tablespoons fish sauce

2 teaspoons sugar

1 teaspoon chili-garlic sauce

½ pound medium shrimp, peeled and deveined, or ½ pound catfish fillets cut into 2-inch chunks

1 cup pineapple chunks, canned or fresh

4 plum tomatoes, cored and quartered

2 tablespoons thinly sliced green onion

2 tablespoons chopped fresh cilantro

GARNISHES (OPTIONAL)

2 tablespoons chopped rice paddy herb (*rau ngo om;* see page 15)

2 tablespoons chopped fresh mint

2 tablespoons chopped fresh Asian or any other type of basil

1 cup mung bean sprouts

To prepare the lemongrass, trim away and discard any dried root portion (to make a smooth base), the top half of the stalks, and any dry, tired outer leaves. Cut the remaining portion of each stalk diagonally into 2-inch lengths.

Combine the oil, garlic, and lemongrass chunks in a large saucepan over medium-high heat and heat until the lemongrass and garlic release their fragrance. Toss for 1 minute and add the broth, tamarind liquid, fish sauce, sugar, and chili-garlic sauce. Bring to a boil, reduce the heat to maintain the soup at a lively simmer, and cook for 10 minutes, stirring once.

Increase the heat to medium-high, and when the soup returns to a boil, add the shrimp, pineapple chunks, and tomatoes and stir well. Cook for 1 to 2 minutes until shrimp are cooked. Stir in the green onion and cilantro, and remove from the heat. Stir in the additional herbs and bean sprouts, if you are using them. Transfer to a serving bowl and serve at once.

SERVES 4

CRAB AND ASPARAGUS SOUP

sup mang tay

This lovely soup is a French colonial creation that showcases asparagus in a standard Chinese-style egg-flower soup. The original version was made with canned asparagus, but you can enjoy the vivid green color and flavor of fresh asparagus, known in Vietnam as *mang tay*, or "Western bamboo." To prepare with canned asparagus (green or white), drain, cut into 1-inch lengths, and add at the end of cooking, just before the egg. I sometimes like to use zucchini, edamame beans (fresh soybeans), baby spinach leaves, or frozen peas in place of asparagus. Canned crabmeat works nicely in this soup, making it an everyday dish.

½ pound fresh asparagus

1 tablespoon vegetable oil

2 tablespoons finely chopped shallots or onion

1 tablespoon finely chopped garlic

½ teaspoon salt

¼ teaspoon black pepper

4 cups chicken broth

2 teaspoons cornstarch

2 tablespoons water

1 egg, well beaten

¼ pound cooked lump crabmeat, or one 6-ounce can, drained (about ¾ cup)

2 tablespoons thinly sliced green onion

Trim the asparagus, breaking off and discarding the base of each stalk about where the bright green color fades. Cut each stalk crosswise diagonally into 1-inch pieces, but leave the beautiful tips intact. (You should have about 2 cups.)

Heat the oil in a medium saucepan over medium-high heat for 1 minute, and then add the asparagus, shallots, garlic, salt, and pepper. Cook until the shallots and garlic are fragrant and the asparagus is shiny and bright green, 1 to 2 minutes. Add the broth and bring to a boil.

In a small bowl, combine the cornstarch and water, stirring it to make a thin, smooth paste. Add it to the soup. Stir the soup well and drizzle in the beaten egg, letting it swirl to form lacy shreds in the hot broth. Add the crabmeat and stir well. Sprinkle in the green onion, remove the soup from the heat, and serve hot or warm.

CHICKEN & EGGS

Chicken is beloved in Vietnamese kitchens, and this chapter gives you lots of ways to enjoy it, from luxurious curry in coconut sauce to poached chicken Hainan-style, served with a vibrant lime sauce and rice cooked in the chicken's ginger-infused broth. I especially like the first dish in this chapter, Lemongrass Chicken, or *ga xao xa ot* (page 54). Like many Vietnamese stir-fried dishes, it showcases the chicken on its own merits rather than using it as one element in a vegetable-and-meat combination. In Chicken Stir-Fried with Fresh Ginger (page 55), the chicken provides a similarly strong flavor note. It is perfect with rice, couscous, polenta, or bread for soaking up every bit of gingery sauce.

You will also find a couple of omelets, which are enjoyed in Vietnam morning, noon, and night. Serve an omelet with rice and Everyday Dipping Sauce (page 156) as one of many dishes composing a meal, or accompany it with only a warm baguette. One omelet is hearty, the other is elegantly divine; one says "yummy" and the other "time for brunch!" I don't know whether the chicken came before the egg, but I do know you will enjoy these Vietnamese classics while you sort it out.

SERVES 4

LEMONGRASS CHICKEN

ga xao xa ot

This simple dish packs a trio of Vietnamese flavors into a quick stir-fry: a bouquet of lemongrass, a salty bass note of fish sauce and garlic, and a sassy little chili kick. To prepare the lemongrass, trim to about 4 inches from the rounded base and discard the grassy tops and any very dry and brown outer portions. Slice the lemongrass crosswise into thin rounds, and then mince them. Or check the freezer at your Asian market for wonderful finely ground and then frozen lemongrass, imported from Vietnam. Serve this dish with rice or noodles so you can savor the delicious sauce.

¾ pound boneless chicken thighs, cut into generous bite-sized chunks, or boneless chicken breasts, cut into strips

2 teaspoons finely chopped garlic

2 tablespoons fish sauce

1 tablespoon soy sauce

2 teaspoons sugar

1 teaspoon cornstarch

¼ cup chopped onion

2 stalks fresh lemongrass, trimmed and chopped

½ cup water or chicken broth

2 tablespoons vegetable oil

½ teaspoon salt

¼ to ½ teaspoon dried red chili flakes

In a medium bowl, combine the chicken with the garlic, 1 tablespoon of the fish sauce, the soy sauce, sugar, and cornstarch. Mix well, and set aside for 15 to 20 minutes. Or cover and refrigerate for up to 1 day.

Combine the onion, lemongrass, and water in a mini–food processor or a blender and process until fairly smooth.

Heat the oil in a medium skillet over medium heat until very hot. Add the marinated chicken and toss well. Add the lemongrass mixture and cook, tossing often, until the chicken changes color. Add the salt and chili flakes, along with the remaining tablespoon of fish sauce, and cook, tossing now and then, until the chicken is cooked, 3 to 4 minutes. Transfer to a serving dish and serve hot or warm.

CHICKEN STIR-FRIED WITH FRESH GINGER

ga xao gung

Toss a few ingredients with strips of chicken, give them a few turns in a hot pan, and you have a flavor-filled dish to serve with rice or toss with noodles. If you have any left, tuck it into a small baguette the next day, along with a tangle of pickled carrots and a sprinkling of fresh herbs, and you'll have *Banh Mi* (page 38), a fabulous sub sandwich for lunch.

2 tablespoons fish sauce

1 tablespoon soy sauce

1 tablespoon honey or brown sugar

½ teaspoon salt

¼ teaspoon black pepper

¾ pound boneless chicken thighs or chicken breasts, cut into long thin strips

2 tablespoons vegetable oil

2 tablespoons finely chopped fresh ginger

2 tablespoons finely chopped green onion

In a medium bowl, combine the fish sauce, soy sauce, honey, salt, and pepper, and stir to mix everything well. Add the chicken, and toss to coat with the seasonings. Set aside for 15 to 20 minutes, or cover and refrigerate for up to 1 day.

Heat the oil in a medium skillet over high heat until a bit of ginger sizzles at once. Add chicken and marinade and cook until the chicken is golden brown on one side, 1 to 2 minutes. Toss well, add the ginger, and toss again. Cook, tossing occasionally, until the chicken is nicely browned and cooked through, 5 to 7 minutes. Transfer to a serving dish, sprinkle with the green onions, and serve hot or warm.

SERVES 6 TO 8

CHICKEN CURRY WITH SWEET POTATOES AND LIME-PEPPER-SALT DIPPING SAUCE

ca ri ga

Make this curry and enjoy it in traditional Vietnamese style, accompanied by a warm, crusty baguette, perfect for dipping in the luscious and fragrant sauce. It's also wonderful with rice and other dishes, as well as over cooked rice noodles in a big bowl. Vietnamese cooks make it with potatoes, taro root, and carrots, as well as sweet potatoes. I love it with chunks of butternut squash or *kabocha,* a small pumpkin with a bumpy greenish orange skin.

If you want to prepare *ca ri ga* in advance, omit the sweet potatoes and add them when you reheat the curry, cooking them until they are tender. You'll find the curry flavors blossom wonderfully when the sauce has the chance to sit overnight in the refrigerator.

2 tablespoons vegetable oil

1 tablespoon coarsely chopped garlic

1 cup sliced onion or shallots

2 stalks fresh lemongrass, trimmed and cut into 2-inch lengths

5 slices fresh ginger

3 tablespoons curry powder

1 ½ pounds whole bone-in chicken thighs or legs, or 1 pound boneless chicken breasts or thighs, cut into big bite-sized chunks

2 tablespoons fish sauce

1 teaspoon sugar

½ teaspoon salt

1 teaspoon dried red chili flakes or chili-garlic sauce

2 ¾ cups chicken broth or water

1 ½ cups unsweetened coconut milk (one 14-ounce can)

2 ½ cups chunks of peeled sweet potatoes or carrots

Lime-Pepper-Salt Dipping Sauce (page 158)**, or 2 tablespoons freshly squeezed lime juice**

continued

In a large, deep saucepan or Dutch oven, heat the oil over medium-high heat for 1 minute. Add the garlic, onion, lemongrass, and ginger and toss well. Add the curry powder and cook, tossing often, until the herbs are fragrant and the onion is translucent, 1 to 2 minutes.

Add the chicken, spreading it out in one layer if you can, and cook for 1 minute. Toss well, and cook until the chicken changes color and begins to brown. Add the fish sauce, sugar, salt, and chili flakes and toss again. Add the broth and bring to a boil. Reduce the heat to maintain a lively simmer, and cook for 10 minutes, stirring now and then.

Add the coconut milk and sweet potatoes and simmer until the sweet potatoes are tender and the chicken is cooked, 10 to 15 minutes. Remove the lemongrass chunks, transfer the chicken and sauce to a serving bowl, and serve hot or warm. Provide a tiny dish of Lime-Pepper-Salt Dipping Sauce for each guest. (Or stir the lime juice into the curry right after removing the lemongrass chunks.)

OMELET WITH CRABMEAT AND GREEN ONIONS

trung chien voi cua

Eggs aren't just for breakfast in Vietnam, and that means more chances to enjoy speedy, satisfying inspirations like this little omelet. It's worthy of center stage at lunchtime, or a costarring role at supper with rice and other dishes. The omelet is fabulous with Everyday Dipping Sauce (page 156) and a warm baguette. For brunch, accompany it with fresh pineapple, biscuits and honey, and steaming cups of sweet, strong coffee, Vietnamese style (page 154).

4 eggs

1 tablespoon fish sauce

2 tablespoons vegetable oil

¼ pound cooked lump crabmeat, or one 6-ounce can, drained (about ¾ cup)

1 tablespoon thinly sliced green onion

¼ teaspoon salt

Generous pinch of black pepper

In a medium bowl, combine the eggs and fish sauce, beat well, and set aside.

Heat 1 tablespoon of the oil in a medium skillet over medium-high heat for 1 minute. Add the crabmeat, green onion, salt, and pepper, and cook, tossing gently, until heated and fragrant, 1 to 2 minutes. Transfer to a small bowl and place by the stove.

Add the remaining tablespoon of oil to the pan and heat until a bit of egg sizzles and blooms at once. Add the eggs and cook, gently pulling the cooked egg toward the center of the pan so that most of the uncooked egg spreads out in the hot pan. When the omelet is lightly browned on the bottom and fairly set on top, spread the crabmeat mixture over half. Gently fold the other half over the crab-covered side, and transfer to a plate. Serve hot or warm.

SERVES 4 TO 6

HAINAN CHICKEN AND RICE WITH GINGER-LIME DIPPING SAUCE

com ga; nuoc mam gung

The chunk of southern China known as Hainan Island sits in the center of the Gulf of Tonkin, across the hauntingly beautiful Ha Long Bay from northern Vietnam. Hainan Island's namesake dish is enjoyed all over Southeast Asia. It consists of chunks of perfectly poached chicken, rice cooked in the broth created by cooking the chicken, and a bowl of the same broth to savor on the side. In Vietnam it's easy to find Hainan chicken and rice in restaurants, served with the refreshing herb *rau ram* and a vibrant ginger sauce, *nuoc mam gung*. Each works beautifully to brighten and balance the rich, mild flavors of the dish. You can make this at home with minimal effort and wonderful results. Instead of Ginger-Lime Dipping Sauce, you could serve the chicken with Everyday Dipping Sauce (page 156), Hoisin-Peanut Dipping Sauce (page 159), or Lime-Pepper-Salt Dipping Sauce (page 158).

FOR THE CHICKEN

3 pounds boneless chicken breasts

6 cups chicken broth

10 slices fresh ginger

2 teaspoons salt

Ginger-Lime Dipping Sauce (page 157) **or Lime-Pepper-Salt Dipping Sauce** (page 158)

FOR THE RICE

3 tablespoons vegetable oil or rendered chicken fat

1 tablespoon chopped garlic

5 thin slices or 2 tablespoons finely chopped fresh ginger

2 cups long-grain rice, such as jasmine

1 teaspoon salt

In a 3-quart saucepan with a tight-fitting lid, combine the chicken with the broth, ginger, and salt. Bring to a boil over medium heat, and then adjust the heat to maintain a gentle simmer. Cook, skimming the broth now and then to remove any foam that rises to the surface, until the chicken is cooked through but still tender, about 25 minutes. While chicken cooks, prepare the Ginger-Lime Dipping Sauce and set aside until serving time.

When the chicken is cooked, transfer it to a bowl or platter to cool. Measure out 2 ¼ cups of the chicken broth and set it aside for cooking the rice. (You can serve any remaining broth alongside the rice, in small bowls, garnished with sliced green onions, or save it for another meal.)

To prepare the rice, heat the oil in a medium saucepan over medium-high heat for 1 minute. Add the garlic and ginger and cook for 1 minute, tossing once or twice. Add the rice and salt and cook, stirring often, until the rice is shiny and white, 2 to 3 minutes. Add the reserved chicken broth, stir well, and bring to a lively boil. Reduce the heat to maintain a gentle simmer, cover, and cook, stirring now and then, until the rice is done, 20 to 25 minutes. Remove from the heat and let stand for 10 minutes or so. Meanwhile, chop the chicken into big chunks, about 2 x 1 inches.

To serve, place the chicken and the small bowl of Ginger-Lime Sauce on one side of a serving platter, and mound the rice on the other side. Serve hot, warm, or at room temperature.

SERVES 4 TO 6

CHICKEN SIMMERED IN CARAMEL SAUCE

thit ga kho gung

After you've made this lovely dish, you'll understand why the clay pot cooking method called *kho* holds such a beloved place on the Vietnamese table. Pork, chicken, fish steaks, and even shrimp are all cooked in this manner: simmered until tender and permeated with a luxurious, reddish brown essence of caramelized sugar and salty fish sauce, spiked with black pepper or chilies. By simmering substantial ingredients such as meat or fish in a clay pot, Vietnamese cooks create enormous flavor for a hungry family while economizing on food and fuel. You will adore this dish, whether you make it as I do in a small sturdy saucepan or a deep skillet on a conventional stove, or in a traditional clay pot on a charcoal stove.

1 ½ pounds boneless chicken thighs

2 tablespoons vegetable oil

1 tablespoon chopped garlic

3 tablespoons finely chopped fresh ginger

2 tablespoons chopped shallots or onion

2 tablespoons fish sauce

2 tablespoons brown sugar or palm sugar

1 tablespoon granulated sugar

½ teaspoon salt

½ teaspoon black pepper

1 teaspoon dried red chili flakes

¼ cup water

3 green onions, trimmed and cut into 2-inch lengths

Chop the chicken into big chunks by halving each thigh and then cutting each half into quarters. In a large, deep skillet or a large saucepan, heat the oil over medium-high heat until a bit of garlic sizzles at once. Add the chicken and cook for about 2 minutes, tossing once or twice.

Push the meat out to the sides of the pan and add the ginger, shallots, and garlic to the middle of the pan. Cook for about 1 minute, and then toss well. Add the fish sauce, both kinds of sugar, the salt, pepper, and chili flakes and toss to mix everything well. Let the sauce come to a strong boil and begin to thicken, and then add the water. Adjust the heat to maintain a lively simmer and then cook the chicken for 10 to 15 minutes, tossing now and then. When the sauce is a handsome reddish brown syrup and the chicken is cooked, add the green onions and toss well. Transfer to a serving dish and serve hot or warm.

SERVES 4 TO 6

FIVE-SPICE ROAST CHICKEN

ga ngu vi huong

The rich, handsome color of Five-Spice Roast Chicken promises a deep, inviting flavor. One bite and I think you will agree that it delivers on that promise. You can roast a whole chicken or small Cornish hens in this way, but I love to cook this with chicken legs and thighs. If you like, serve this hot from the oven along with Sticky Rice (page 117) and an array of dishes. Use any leftovers in Summer Rolls (page 31) or in *Banh Mi* Submarine Sandwiches (page 38).

¼ cup soy sauce

2 tablespoons fish sauce

1 tablespoon Asian sesame oil

1 tablespoon brown sugar or granulated sugar

2 teaspoons five-spice powder

½ teaspoon salt

1 tablespoon finely chopped garlic

2 teaspoons finely chopped ginger

3 ½ pounds bone-in chicken legs and thighs, or chicken wings

Combine the soy sauce, fish sauce, sesame oil, sugar, five-spice powder, and salt in a large bowl and stir to mix well. Stir in the garlic and ginger, and then add the chicken pieces, turning to coat all sides with the marinade. Cover and refrigerate for at least 1 hour, or overnight. Turn the pieces now and then so that the marinade coats them evenly.

To cook the chicken, preheat the oven to 375°F. Place the chicken in a roasting pan and roast, until it is richly browned and cooked through, 30 to 45 minutes. Transfer to a serving platter and serve hot, warm, or at room temperature.

SERVES 4 TO 6

OMELET WITH BEAN THREAD NOODLES AND PORK

cha trung

Order *com tam bi* in a Vietnamese café serving rice dishes, and you'll get a fabulous feast of rice along with shredded pork, peppery pork chops, and a chunk of this tasty omelet, which is called *cha trung* when served by itself. It's meaty and hearty, great with rice and other dishes, Vietnamese style. You can bake this in a 9-inch square or round cake pan, or a loaf pan, and then cut it into squares or wedges after it has cooled.

About 2 ounces dried bean thread noodles

About ⅓ cup dried cloud ear mushrooms, or 5 dried Chinese mushrooms (optional)

5 eggs

¼ pound ground pork

2 tablespoons fish sauce

½ teaspoon salt

¼ teaspoon black pepper

3 tablespoons finely chopped green onion

2 tablespoons vegetable oil

Put the bean thread noodles in a medium bowl and the dried mushrooms (if using) in a small bowl, and cover each with warm water. Set aside to soften for 10 to 20 minutes.

Meanwhile, beat the eggs in a medium bowl. Add the pork, fish sauce, salt, pepper, and green onion, and then set aside.

When the noodles are soft and clear, drain and then rinse them well with cool water. Transfer to a cutting board and chop into 2-inch lengths. Drain the softened mushrooms, cut away and discard any hard lumps or stems, and cut into thin strips. Add the noodles and mushrooms to the eggs and pork and mix everything together as best you can, breaking up any large clumps of pork.

Heat the oil in a medium skillet over high heat until a drop of egg sizzles and blooms at once. Add the egg mixture, lower the heat to medium, and cook for 3 to 4 minutes. As the omelet begins to set, use a spoon to work your way around the pan, pulling the cooked edges toward the center so that some of the uncooked egg spreads out in the hot pan.

Gently slide the half-cooked omelet onto a plate, place the hot pan upside down over the uncooked surface of the omelet, and invert the plate so that the cooked side faces up. Return the pan to the heat and continue cooking the omelet until the meat is done and the omelet is golden brown on both sides, 2 to 3 minutes. Transfer to a serving plate and serve hot, warm, or at room temperature.

BEEF & PORK

Beef is such a big deal in Vietnam that it has its own ritual: the special occasion restaurant meal known as *bo bay mon.* It's translated as "seven-course beef" or "beef seven ways," and if you see it featured at a Vietnamese dining establishment, I recommend you treat yourself. This chapter doesn't quite have seven courses of beef, but it comes close. And Vietnam's pork dishes are so beloved, they are not to be left in the shadow for lack of their own restaurant legend.

Delicious Lemongrass Burgers (page 71) are fabulous with either pork or beef. Pork in Caramel Sauce (page 80) is a classic southern braise that seems impossibly good for something so easy to prepare. If you can call in some helpers, put on a little grill fest featuring Grilled Pork Patties with Lettuce, Noodles, Peanuts, and Mint, Hanoi Style (page 76). It's my version of the street-food standout, *bun cha ha noi.* Once you have the grill going, why not put together a few skewers of Lemongrass Beef (page 68), so that you have lots of smoke-kissed flavors to share with friends.

SERVES 4 TO 6

LEMONGRASS BEEF, GRILLED OR SAUTÉED

bo nuong xa

Lemongrass beef is definitely on the short list of almost-irresistible Vietnamese dishes. You can grill the beef on skewers, restaurant style, or quickly sauté it in a hot pan and get it on the table fast. I enjoy using lemongrass beef in place of the roast chicken for Big, Cool Noodle Bowl (page 133), transforming it into the Vietnamese noodle classic *bun bo xa.* You will need 2 to 3 stalks of fresh lemongrass, trimmed (see page 19) and chopped. Finely ground lemongrass is now available frozen in small and large containers imported from Vietnam. Convenient and of high quality, it's perfect for busy days, or anytime fresh lemongrass is difficult to find.

1 pound boneless beef, such as tri-tip or sirloin tip

3 tablespoons finely chopped fresh lemongrass

1 tablespoon chopped garlic

1 tablespoon chopped shallots or onion

2 tablespoons fish sauce

1 tablespoon sugar

1 teaspoon soy sauce

1 teaspoon Asian sesame oil

15 to 20 bamboo skewers, soaked in water for at least 30 minutes

Slice the beef thinly into strips about 2 inches long and put in a medium bowl. Combine the lemongrass, garlic, shallots, fish sauce, sugar, soy sauce, and sesame oil in a mini–food processor or a blender and blend until fairly smooth. (Add a little water if needed to move the blades.) Transfer the marinade to the bowl, toss the beef to coat evenly, and set aside for 30 minutes to 1 hour, or cover and refrigerate for up to 1 day.

To cook the beef, thread it onto bamboo skewers, pushing pieces together to fill most of the skewer, and leaving about 2 inches at each end. Build a hot charcoal fire or preheat a gas grill or the broiler. To grill, place the skewers on the hot grill and cook for 1 to 2 minutes on each side, using tongs or a long-handled spatula and grill fork to move the skewers off the grill as soon as they are done. To broil, place the skewers in a roasting pan and slide under the broiler until cooked, 1 to 2 minutes per side. You could also sauté the marinated beef quickly in a hot pan with 2 tablespoons of oil, turning once. Transfer the beef to a serving platter and serve hot or warm.

SERVES 4

BEEF STIR-FRIED WITH ASPARAGUS

bo xao mang tay

Although Vietnamese cooks usually prepare meat and vegetables separately, they sometimes stir-fry them together, just as people do in China and throughout Southeast Asia. Beef is often paired with cauliflower or broccoli florets, thin slices of bamboo or celery, or asparagus. This dish cooks in a flash, each component complementing the other and inviting you to cook a pot of rice and pull up a chair. There is not much sauce, but the flavors are simple and clear. At my house we add a bowl of Everyday Dipping Sauce (page 156) for a fast, satisfying meal, but in Vietnam this would be one of many dishes served at a rice-centered meal.

¼ pound boneless beef, such as flank steak, tri-tip, or sirloin, thinly sliced

2 tablespoons fish sauce

1 tablespoon soy sauce

½ teaspoon black pepper

½ teaspoon sugar

½ pound asparagus, broccoli florets, or 3 or 4 stalks celery

2 tablespoons vegetable oil

1 tablespoon chopped garlic

2 tablespoons water

2 tablespoons thinly sliced green onion

In a medium bowl, combine the beef with 1 tablespoon of the fish sauce, the soy sauce, black pepper, and sugar, and toss to mix well. Set aside for 15 to 20 minutes while you prepare the remaining ingredients.

Trim the asparagus, breaking off the grayish base of each stalk, and cutting the green upper portion diagonally into 2-inch lengths. (Or cut the broccoli florets into bite-sized pieces. Or trim both ends of the celery stalks and pull off the stringy outer layer with a paring knife or a vegetable peeler, then cut diagonally into thin pieces.) You should have about 2 cups of chopped or sliced vegetables. Set aside.

In a large skillet or a wok, heat the oil over high heat for 30 seconds. Add the garlic, toss well, and then scatter the beef in the pan. Cook briefly on one side, then toss once to sear the other side. Add the asparagus and toss well. Add the remaining tablespoon of fish sauce, the water, and the green onion. Cook, tossing once or twice, until the asparagus is shiny and tender, but not soft, about 1 minute. Transfer to a serving dish and serve hot or warm.

DELICIOUS LEMONGRASS BURGERS WITH BEEF OR PORK

bo nuong xa; cha heo

A handful of inspired Vietnamese seasonings can make your same old burger extraordinary. Make this with beef, and you have one of the parade of beef dishes composing *bo bay mon,* a special-occasion feast originating in northern Vietnam. Use ground pork, and you have *cha heo,* a lemongrass-infused patty enjoyed as a street-food snack throughout the Mekong Delta. This recipe makes a dozen snack-sized burgers, great for wrapping in lettuce-and-herb packets for dipping, or simply for nibbling along with other starters. If you prefer, you can make two dozen meatballs, or double the recipe to make four standard-size burgers.

½ pound ground beef or pork

2 tablespoons finely chopped fresh lemongrass

2 tablespoons finely chopped green onion

2 tablespoons finely chopped fresh cilantro

1 tablespoon finely chopped garlic

1 tablespoon vegetable oil

1 tablespoon fish sauce

2 teaspoons soy sauce

½ teaspoon sugar

½ teaspoon salt

¼ teaspoon black pepper

ACCOMPANIMENTS

Everyday Dipping Sauce (page 156)

Everyday Herb and Salad Plate (page 100)**, made with lettuce cups, cilantro, and mint**

In a medium bowl, combine the ground beef with the lemongrass, green onion, cilantro, garlic, oil, fish sauce, soy sauce, sugar, salt, and pepper, and mix well. Set aside to season for at least 15 minutes, or refrigerate for as long as 1 day.

Build a hot charcoal fire or preheat a gas grill or the broiler. Divide the meat mixture into 12 chunks and shape each into a small patty about 2 inches in diameter. Cook on the hot grill until nicely browned and cooked to your liking, 3 to 4 minutes on each side. To broil, place in a roasting pan and slide under the broiler until cooked, 3 to 4 minutes per side. You could also cook the patties quickly in a hot pan with 1 or 2 tablespoons of oil, turning once. Serve hot, warm, or at room temperature, with Everyday Dipping Sauce and Everyday Herb and Salad Plate, so guests can make small bundles for dipping into the sauce.

SERVES 4

SHAKING BEEF WITH PURPLE ONIONS AND WATERCRESS

bo luc lac

A few easy steps and you'll have a hearty centerpiece for a quick meal with rice, or a spectacular starter. You can use fresh spinach instead of watercress, tearing any large leaves into bite-sized pieces, or try the packaged lettuce mixtures in the produce section. Use any kind of vinegar you like, and try serving Shaking Beef with little saucers of Lime-Pepper-Salt Dipping Sauce (page 158) for an extra burst of flavor.

FOR THE MARINATED BEEF

¾ pound thickly cut steak, such as New York strip or rib eye

1 tablespoon fish sauce

2 teaspoons soy sauce

½ teaspoon sugar

½ teaspoon black pepper

2 tablespoons vegetable oil

2 tablespoons finely chopped garlic

FOR THE WATERCRESS SALAD

2 tablespoons vinegar

1 teaspoon vegetable oil

1 teaspoon sugar

½ teaspoon salt

½ teaspoon black pepper

½ cup very thin onion slices, preferably purple onion

2 cups bite-sized or torn pieces of watercress, tender spinach, or lettuce leaves

continued

To marinate the beef, begin by cutting it into big, bite-sized chunks, about 1 inch square. In a medium bowl, combine the fish sauce, soy sauce, sugar, and pepper and stir well. Add the beef, toss to coat it evenly, and set aside for 20 to 30 minutes while you make the salad. Or cover and refrigerate for up to 1 day.

To make the watercress salad, combine the vinegar, oil, sugar, salt, and pepper in a medium bowl and stir well. Add the thinly sliced onion and toss to coat it with the dressing. Add the watercress to the bowl but don't toss it yet.

To cook the beef, heat the oil in a large, heavy skillet over high heat until a bit of garlic sizzles at once. Add the beef and let it cook on one side, undisturbed, until nicely browned, 1 to 2 minutes. Shake the pan to turn the meat and cook the other surface the same way. Add the garlic and continue cooking, shaking and searing the meat, until evenly browned and done to your liking. Remove the pan from the heat and set aside while you prepare the serving platter.

Toss the watercress to coat it with the dressing and arrange it on a small serving platter. Scoop up the steak, pile it in the center of the watercress salad, and serve hot or warm.

SERVES 6

VIETNAMESE MEAT LOAF

cha dum

Make this satisfying dish over the weekend, and you can enjoy it in quick hearty meals during the week. Vietnamese-style meat loaf makes a fine addition to Submarine Sandwiches, Saigon Style (page 38), or a Big, Cool Noodle Bowl (page 133). In Vietnamese kitchens, *cha dum* takes many forms, every one of them delicious. It's often steamed in a small bowl, rather than baked. Then it's inverted onto a plate, sliced, and served with an array of side-dishes and rice. You could also shape the mixture into big meatballs for steaming or pan-frying. Look for *cha dum* as part of the popular Vietnamese celebration meal *bo bay mon,* or "seven-course beef." The dried mushrooms and bean thread noodles add texture and amplify the flavors, but you'll have a tasty dish even if you leave them out.

5 dried Chinese mushrooms (optional)

1 to 2 ounces dried bean thread noodles (optional)

1 pound ground beef or pork, or a mixture of both

2 tablespoons finely chopped onion or shallots

1 tablespoon finely chopped garlic

2 tablespoons fish sauce

½ teaspoon salt

½ teaspoon black pepper

1 egg, well beaten

Put the Chinese mushrooms and bean thread noodles, if using, in separate bowls and cover each with warm water. Set aside for 10 to 20 minutes, or until flexible enough to cut. Drain both ingredients and transfer to a cutting board. Cut away any hard lumps or stems, and chop the mushroom caps into small pieces. Pile up the noodles and coarsely chop them as well.

Preheat the oven to 375°F. In a medium bowl combine the meat with the onion, garlic, fish sauce, salt, pepper, egg, and the chopped mushrooms and noodles. Mix with your hands or two large spoons to combine everything well. Transfer to a small loaf pan, pie pan, or heat-proof bowl.

Bake the meat loaf until firm, fragrant, and cooked through, 30 to 40 minutes. Or place the pan on the tray of a steamer, described on page 22, and steam for 30 to 40 minutes. Set the meat loaf aside to cool for 10 minutes or so and then transfer to a serving platter and serve hot, warm, or at room temperature. (Or cool to room temperature, cover, and refrigerate for up to 2 days.)

SERVES 6 TO 8

GRILLED PORK PATTIES WITH LETTUCE, NOODLES, PEANUTS, AND MINT, HANOI STYLE

bun cha ha noi

Incredibly delicious and easy, this brilliant dish is a street-food classic originating in northern Vietnam. The real thing can be had from sidewalk vendors and open-air shops specializing in *bun cha ha noi,* where customers flock as soon as the day's first batch fills the air with its signature grill-fired aroma, an irresistible olfactory invitation. While this home version can't deliver the atmosphere, it makes for a memorable feast and takes only a few minutes to prepare. For a classic presentation, immerse the grilled patties and pork strips in a bowl of Everyday Dipping Sauce (page 156) for a few minutes. Then provide each guest with chopsticks or a fork and a small bowl in which to combine the pork with the accompaniments, or serve the meat hot off the grill with hot sauce or barbecue sauce, or with bowls of Everyday Dipping Sauce, a plate of cucumber slices, and Sticky Rice (page 117). Look for fresh bacon, or belly pork, at the butcher counter in large Asian markets.

FOR THE GRILLED PORK AND PORK PATTIES

2 tablespoons fish sauce

2 tablespoons Caramel Sauce (page 158) **or brown sugar**

2 teaspoons vegetable oil

1 teaspoon salt

1 teaspoon black pepper

½ pound fresh bacon or any boneless pork, sliced ¼ inch thick and cut into 3-inch pieces

½ pound ground pork

¼ cup finely chopped green onion

ACCOMPANIMENTS

¼ pound thin dried rice noodles, soaked in warm water to cover for 20 minutes or more

Double recipe Everyday Dipping Sauce (page 156; about 1 cup)

Everyday Pickled Carrots (page 108)

3 cups shredded lettuce leaves

½ cup fresh mint leaves

½ cup fresh cilantro leaves

½ cup chopped roasted and salted peanuts

continued

To prepare the meat, combine the fish sauce, Caramel Sauce, oil, salt, and pepper in a small bowl or cup, and stir to mix everything well. Put the sliced pork in one medium bowl, and the ground pork in another, and divide the marinade between the two. Turn the sliced pork to coat it evenly and set aside. Add the green onion to the ground pork and its marinade and mix well. Set both bowls aside for 20 to 30 minutes while you prepare the accompaniments, or cover and refrigerate for up to 1 day.

To prepare the accompaniments, bring a medium saucepan of water to a rolling boil over high heat. Drain the noodles and then drop them into the boiling water. Remove the pan from the heat at once and set aside for 10 minutes. Drain, rinse with cool water, drain well again, and set aside. Prepare all the remaining accompaniments and arrange them on serving platters.

When you are ready to serve *bun cha ha noi,* build a hot charcoal fire or preheat a gas grill. Shape the ground pork into small patties, using about 2 tablespoons for each one. Set aside on a platter, and drain the marinated sliced pork and place alongside them. Cook the sliced pork and patties on the hot grill, turning once or twice, until pleasingly browned and cooked through. (You could also cook the pork in 2 tablespoons of vegetable oil in a very hot skillet; or roast in a hot oven until the meat is nicely browned and cooked through.)

Transfer the meat to a serving platter and serve hot or warm. Give each guest a small bowl of Everyday Dipping Sauce and a bowl in which to mix up the *bun cha* and accompaniments. They may want to soak pork slices and patties in the sauce for a few minutes before eating them, or dip along as they please.

SERVES 4 TO 6

GRILLED GARLIC-PEPPER PORK CHOPS

thit heo nuong vi

Sweet and salty, these pork chops fit any menu and can be grilled or roasted in the oven. You could also use them on *com tam bi,* the classic rice dish popular in Vietnamese restaurants. A sort of blue plate special created to provide a hearty and varied rice meal for people dining alone, *com tam bi* consists of rice topped with thin strips of sweet-and-salty pork chops like these, a hearty portion of Omelet with Bean Thread Noodles and Pork (page 65), and shredded pork seasoned with roasted rice powder. Everyday Dipping Sauce (page 156) and a garnish of lettuce, cucumber, and tomato round out the offerings. If you have leftover Grilled Garlic-Pepper Pork Chops, slice the meat thinly and use it in a Vietnamese submarine sandwich, *banh mi* (page 38).

2 tablespoons fish sauce

1 tablespoon soy sauce

2 tablespoons sugar

1 tablespoon Caramel Sauce (page 158) **or brown sugar**

1 tablespoon vegetable oil

1 tablespoon garlic

½ teaspoon salt

½ teaspoon black pepper

4 to 6 bone-in pork chops (about 2 pounds)

Everyday Dipping Sauce (page 156)

To make a marinade for the pork chops, combine the fish sauce, soy sauce, sugar, Caramel Sauce, oil, garlic, salt, and pepper in a mini–food processor or blender and process until you have a fairly smooth sauce. Combine the marinade with the pork chops in a medium bowl, and turn the chops to coat them evenly. Set aside for 30 minutes to 1 hour, or cover and chill for up to 1 day.

To cook the pork chops, build a hot charcoal fire, preheat a gas grill, or preheat the oven to 400°F. Place the chops on the hot grill and cook until nicely browned and cooked through, turning once or twice. Or roast in the oven until done. Transfer the pork chops to a serving platter and serve whole, or let stand on a cutting board for 10 to 15 minutes, and then cut into strips. Serve hot, warm, or at room temperature with Everyday Dipping Sauce.

SERVES 4 TO 6

PORK IN CARAMEL SAUCE

thit heo kho

Look for this fabulous dish in Vietnamese restaurants, where it is often served right in its small clay cooking pot. Clay pots, called *kho* in Vietnam, are the perfect vessel for this kind of cooking. Meat, fish, or shellfish simmers slowly in a simple sauce that is both salty and sweet. The cook can focus on other things while a little protein, consuming very little fuel, blossoms into lots of flavor and sauce. *Kho* dishes made economic sense in hard times, and they make gastronomic sense any time because they taste so good. Marbled pork with some fat is traditional, but lean pork is delicious as well. Clay pots are lovely, but you can make an outstanding *kho* dish in a small, sturdy saucepan. Caramel Sauce (page 158) is perfect here, but even if you use sugar, you'll still have a wonderful dish. To slice the meat thinly, put it in the freezer for up to an hour before you cut it. Vietnamese cooks often serve this with pickled bean sprouts for a sour counterpoint to the intense sweet-and-salty flavor of the pork and its sauce.

½ pound boneless pork, thinly sliced

3 tablespoons fish sauce

3 tablespoons water

2 tablespoons sugar

1 tablespoon Caramel Sauce (page 158) **or brown sugar**

½ teaspoon black pepper

In a small saucepan or a clay pot, combine the pork, fish sauce, water, sugar, and Caramel Sauce, stir well, and bring to a gentle boil over medium-high heat. Adjust the heat to maintain a lively simmer and cook, stirring often, for 8 to 10 minutes. The sauce should be filled with voluptuous, caramel-colored bubbles blooming among the pork pieces, and the pork should take on a gorgeous, shiny, caramel hue as it cooks through.

When the pork is cooked and the sauce is satiny, remove from the heat and stir in the pepper. Transfer to a small serving dish and serve hot, warm, or at room temperature, ideally with lots of rice.

SERVES 6 TO 8

PORK AND HARD-BOILED EGGS SIMMERED IN COCONUT JUICE

thit kho nuoc dua

This classic dish has roots in Chinese clay pot cooking, but the tropical note of green coconut juice used to braise the meat is pure Vietnamese. If your coconut tree is bare, don't fret. Asian markets often carry fresh, clear coconut juice in cans, both as a refreshing drink and as a cooking ingredient. Look for *nuoc dua tuol* on the label, and don't worry if it includes some pulp—traditional cooks include a little young coconut meat in the dish when working from a plump, green coconut fresh off the tree. If you don't have coconut juice, just use chicken broth or water instead. Marbled pork with some fat included makes for a particularly rich version, but even lean pork will give you a wonderful, substantial dish. Although this dish takes a while to cook, the prep work is easily and quickly done, and then it's a simple matter of letting the pork simmer until your comfort-food stew is ready for savoring, ideally with lots of rice or a wonderful bread. Vietnamese families often include this dish in a feast during Tet, a celebration of the lunar New Year.

1 ½ pounds boneless pork, cut into 3-inch chunks

3 ½ cups coconut juice or chicken broth

3 tablespoons fish sauce

2 tablespoons Caramel Sauce (page 158) **or brown sugar**

1 tablespoon finely chopped shallots or onion

1 teaspoon salt

½ teaspoon black pepper

3 hard-boiled eggs

3 green onions, cut into 2-inch lengths

In a large, heavy saucepan, combine the pork, coconut juice, fish sauce, Caramel Sauce, shallots, salt, and pepper. Bring to a rolling boil over medium-high heat, and then reduce the heat to maintain an active simmer. Cover and cook until the pork is tender and surrounded by a handsome brown sauce, 45 to 50 minutes.

Add the eggs and green onions to the pan, and simmer for another 15 minutes, turning the eggs gently now and then so they turn a handsome brown. Remove from the heat, take out the eggs, and halve them lengthwise. Carefully return the eggs to the sauce, transfer everything to a serving bowl, and serve hot or warm.

FISH & SHELLFISH

In Vietnam, water seems to flow through every aspect of life. Veined with streams and rivers and flanked by the ocean along its curving southern and eastern borders, the Vietnamese landscape places its people in relationship to water. No wonder fish and seafood show up so often, and with such inspiration, on the Vietnamese table.

Despite Vietnam's proximity to the ocean, freshwater fish are more common fare than saltwater fish and shellfish. This reflects both economics and preference. Harvesting the ocean's bounty takes long hours, big boats, and many hands, while catfish, snakehead, and mullet can be had for a stroll to the riverbank and a brief fishing session. The Vietnamese preference for freshness is reflected here as well. If they don't catch the fish themselves, they buy it at the daily market from a local vendor who did.

These recipes offer an array of dishes illustrating the Vietnamese approach to cooking fish and shellfish. Freshwater fish stars in *Cha Ca* Fish with Fresh Dill, Hanoi Style (page 89), the signature dish of the venerable restaurant Cha Ca La Vong. My version offers a delicious taste of this grilled tour de force, streamlined for cooking at home. Salmon stars in both Grilled Salmon with Chili-Lime Sauce (page 94) and Salmon Steaks in Caramel Fish Sauce (page 96). Both show off salmon's color and flavor, but either could be made with almost any firm-fleshed fish.

Three shrimp dishes complete the picture, one grilled and two simmered. All of the recipes in this chapter offer you ways to create bright and varied dishes inspired by experts, the accomplished cooks of fish-and-seafood-loving Vietnam.

SERVES 4

GRILLED TUNA STEAKS WITH PINEAPPLE-CHILI SAUCE

ca nuong vi; nuoc mam nem

Don't settle for good fast food when you can have great food fast. The tuna is simple and tasty, and the sauce is fantastic. It's a simplified version of *mam nem*, a pungent dipping sauce made with anchovies and pineapple that Vietnamese cooks pair with grilled and fried foods, particularly fish. I suggest anchovy paste here, but you could substitute fish sauce or chopped anchovies and still have a terrific sauce. Or serve your tuna steaks with Everyday Dipping Sauce (page 156), the inspired Vietnamese go-with-everything table sauce known as *nuoc cham*.

FOR THE FISH

2 tablespoons fish sauce

1 tablespoon soy sauce

1 tablespoon vegetable oil

1 teaspoon sugar

¼ teaspoon black pepper

1 ¼ pounds tuna steaks, or salmon, mackerel, or bluefish fillets or steaks

FOR THE PINEAPPLE-CHILI SAUCE

⅓ cup fresh or canned pineapple chunks or drained crushed pineapple

3 tablespoons freshly squeezed lime juice

2 tablespoons chopped green onion

2 tablespoons chopped fresh cilantro

2 tablespoons sugar

1 tablespoon anchovy paste, chopped anchovies, or fish sauce

2 teaspoons minced garlic

½ teaspoon chili-garlic sauce or chopped fresh hot chilies

continued

To marinate the fish, combine the fish sauce, soy sauce, oil, sugar, and pepper in a medium bowl and stir to dissolve the sugar. Place the fish steaks in the bowl, turn to coat them well, and let them marinate for 20 to 30 minutes, turning once. Cover and refrigerate for up to 1 day if you won't be cooking the fish right away.

To prepare the Pineapple-Chili Sauce, combine the pineapple, lime juice, green onion, cilantro, sugar, anchovy paste, garlic, and chili-garlic sauce in a mini–food processor or blender, and blend until fairly smooth. Transfer to a small bowl and set aside until serving time.

To cook the fish, build a hot charcoal fire, preheat a gas grill, or preheat the oven to 375°F. Place the fish steaks carefully on the grill and cook for about 5 minutes on each side, or until cooked through. Or bake for about 15 minutes. Transfer to a serving platter, add the bowl of Pineapple-Chili Sauce, and serve hot or warm.

SERVES 4 TO 6

SHRIMP AND RICE PORRIDGE WITH CILANTRO AND TOMATOES

chao tom

Don't wait for a sick day to make this satisfying and beautiful dish. Rice porridge simmers away all over Asia. Each cuisine makes its own particular improvements to the genre, but each version possesses the defining qualities of hot, thick, salty, soothing, and welcome anytime, day or night. In Vietnam, the shrimp go in early and cook along with the rice, but I like the delicate texture I get by adding them just before serving. If you have *chao tom* left over, expect it to thicken a lot once it cools down. Reheat it gently, adding a little chicken broth, salt as needed, and a handful of green onions and cilantro to restore its freshly made qualities.

½ pound medium shrimp, peeled, deveined, and coarsely chopped

1 tablespoon finely chopped shallots

1 tablespoon finely chopped garlic

2 tablespoons fish sauce

½ teaspoon black pepper

¼ teaspoon salt

6 cups chicken broth

¾ cup long-grain rice, rinsed and drained

2 tablespoons vegetable oil

1 cup coarsely chopped plum tomatoes (optional)

2 tablespoons thinly sliced green onion

2 tablespoons coarsely chopped fresh cilantro

In a medium bowl, combine the shrimp with the shallots, garlic, fish sauce, pepper, and salt. Toss to mix well and set aside while the rice cooks.

Bring the broth to a rolling boil in a medium saucepan over medium-high heat. Stir in the rice, return to a boil, and then lower the heat to maintain a gentle simmer. Cook until the rice is very soft, about 15 minutes. Remove from the heat and cover to keep warm.

In a medium skillet over medium-high heat, heat the oil until hot. Add the shrimp mixture and cook, tossing well, until the garlic is fragrant and the shrimp are turning pink, 1 to 2 minutes. Transfer the shrimp mixture to the rice, scraping the pan to get out every bit of flavor. Return the porridge to a gentle boil, and cook for 2 to 3 minutes. Stir in the tomatoes (if using), green onion, and cilantro, remove from heat, and serve hot or warm.

SERVES 4

SPEEDY SHRIMP IN CARAMEL-CHILI SAUCE

tom rim

This beautiful, delicious dish is perfect for lighting up a weeknight supper. Accompany with Spinach Sautéed with Garlic and Pepper (page 109) or Everyday Herb and Salad Plate (page 100) and a bowl of rice. You could also toss these shrimp with rice noodles and edamame beans, or with spaghetti and peas, for a pretty and tasty noodle bowl.

2 tablespoons vegetable oil

1 tablespoon finely chopped garlic

¼ cup finely chopped onion

½ pound medium shrimp, peeled and deveined

2 tablespoons fish sauce

1 tablespoon sugar

¼ teaspoon dried red chili flakes

¼ cup water

2 tablespoons thinly sliced green onion

2 tablespoons finely chopped fresh cilantro

Heat the oil in a medium skillet over medium heat until hot. Add the garlic and onion and toss well. Add the shrimp and cook, tossing once, until they turn pink. Stir in the fish sauce, sugar, and chili flakes, and then add the water. Cook, tossing once or twice, until the shrimp are cooked through and the other ingredients combine to make a thin sauce, 2 to 3 minutes. Sprinkle with the green onion and cilantro and toss well. Transfer to a serving dish and serve hot or warm.

SERVES 4

CHA CA FISH WITH FRESH DILL, HANOI STYLE

cha ca ha noi

Imagine a dish so inviting and delicious that it earns a place on the map of a city, and so appealing that it supports a family-run restaurant from one century into the next, through decades of war and times of hardship, right on into the new millennium. That legendary dish is Hanoi's *cha ca,* made with chunks of freshwater fish seasoned with *galanga* (a member of the ginger family) and garlic, colored with turmeric to a warm golden hue, and grilled over charcoal for a smoky note. Then it is fried up with handfuls of fresh dill on a tabletop stove and served over thin rice noodles, shredded lettuce, chopped peanuts, and *nuoc cham*. Customers flock to Cha Ca La Vong, located on Hanoi's Cha Ca Street, just to feast on this unique and venerable dish at its source. My streamlined version of *cha ca* gives you a delicious, aromatic, and gorgeous dish so appealing you will want to make it often, and so easy that you can do just that. You can also omit accompaniments, sprinkle with the chopped peanuts, and serve *cha ca ha noi* as a main dish.

FOR THE MARINADE

2 tablespoons fish sauce

1 tablespoon vegetable oil

1 tablespoon finely minced fresh ginger or fresh or frozen *galanga*

1 teaspoon ground turmeric

¼ teaspoon salt

1 pound firm-fleshed fish fillets, such as catfish, monkfish, or tilapia

ACCOMPANIMENTS

½ pound thin, dried rice noodles, softened in warm water for at least 15 minutes, or angel hair pasta

3 cups shredded lettuce leaves, such as Boston, Bibb, or oak leaf

1 cup fresh mint, cilantro, or Asian basil leaves

½ cup chopped roasted and salted peanuts

Double recipe Everyday Dipping Sauce (page 156) **or Pineapple-Chili Sauce** (page 84)

FOR COOKING THE FISH

2 tablespoons vegetable oil

2 cups coarsely chopped fresh dill

5 green onions, trimmed, white part chopped, and green part cut into 2-inch lengths

continued

To marinate the fish, in a medium bowl, combine the fish sauce, oil, ginger, turmeric, and salt and stir to mix well. Cut the fish into big bite-sized chunks (2 or 3 inches square) and add them to the bowl, tossing to coat well. Set aside while you prepare the noodles and other accompaniments, or cover and chill to marinate for up to 1 day.

To cook the rice noodles, bring a medium saucepan of water to a rolling boil over high heat. Drain the soaked noodles well, drop them into the boiling water, and immediately remove from the heat. Let stand for 10 minutes, drain well, and set aside in a medium bowl. (If using angel hair pasta, cook in boiling salted water until tender but still firm, drain well, and set aside). Prepare the accompaniments so that you can serve fish at once.

To cook the fish, place the oil, dill, and green onions by the stove. Heat the oil in a large, heavy skillet over medium-high heat until a bit of dill sizzles at once. Add the fish to the pan and cook on one side for about 2 minutes. Gently turn and let the fish cook for another minute. Add the dill and green onions to the pan and cook for another minute, tossing gently to wilt the herbs. Transfer to a serving platter.

To serve this dish the classic small-bowl way, start each guest off with a small bowl holding a portion of each accompaniment: noodles, lettuce, and a few leaves of mint, cilantro, or Asian basil. Top with a piece or two of fish with dill and green onions, sprinkle with chopped peanuts, and drizzle with a spoonful of Everyday Dipping Sauce. Invite your guests to continue serving themselves in this way.

To serve the big-noodle-bowl way, divide the accompaniments, fish, dill, and green onions among 4 big noodle bowls or pasta plates. Season each bowl with Everyday Dipping Sauce and invite each guest to toss with chopsticks or a fork and spoon, and enjoy.

SERVES 4; MAKES ABOUT ½ CUP OF SAUCE

GRILLED SHRIMP WITH TAMARIND SAUCE

tom nuong; nuoc cham me

I love the flavor of tamarind, an intense sweet-and-sour essence, which makes a fabulous partner for shrimp. Tamarind liquid is made by soaking, mashing, and straining the ripe, bean-shaped pods of the tamarind tree. You can find tamarind pulp in soft blocks at Asian markets and make tamarind liquid as you need it (see page 20). Or check out the thick, luscious, ready-to-use tamarind liquid widely available among the seasonings in said markets. It offers a welcome shortcut to the pleasures of using tamarind in your kitchen. Years ago tamarind concentrate was sticky, hard, and lacking the complex flavor I adore. Modern versions, such as the Garden Queen brand Concentrate Cooking Tamarind, suit me fine. Look for the Vietnamese words for tamarind liquid, *nuoc me chua,* displayed on the label, and store it in the refrigerator after opening. It's handy but it won't keep forever, so make this yummy sauce a lot. I also use Indian-style tamarind chutney, often available in well-stocked supermarkets as well as South Asian grocery stores, when I need good tamarind flavor fast.

FOR THE TAMARIND SAUCE

1 teaspoon vegetable oil

1 teaspoon minced garlic

⅓ cup prepared tamarind liquid, Indian-style tamarind chutney, or freshly made tamarind liquid (see page 20)

2 tablespoons fish sauce, or 1 teaspoon salt

2 tablespoons water

2 tablespoons granulated sugar

1 tablespoon brown sugar

½ teaspoon black pepper

¼ teaspoon dried red chili flakes or chili-garlic sauce

FOR THE SHRIMP

½ pound medium shrimp, peeled and deveined

1 tablespoon vegetable oil

½ teaspoon salt

¼ teaspoon black pepper

12 to 15 bamboo skewers, soaked in water for at least 30 minutes

To make the Tamarind Sauce, in a small saucepan or skillet, heat the oil and garlic over medium heat until the garlic is fragrant and sizzles, about 1 minute. Add the tamarind liquid, fish sauce, water, granulated sugar, brown sugar, pepper, and chili flakes, and stir well. Cook, stirring often, until the sugars dissolve and the sauce is smooth and thickened a bit, 3 to 5 minutes. Set aside while you cook the shrimp. Serve warm or at room temperature, or transfer to a sealed jar, close tightly, and refrigerate for up to 2 days.

To cook the shrimp, build a hot charcoal fire, preheat a gas grill or the broiler, preheat the oven to 425°F, or lightly oil a skillet or grill pan and heat until very hot. In a medium bowl combine the shrimp, oil, salt, and pepper, and toss to coat well. Set aside for 10 to 15 minutes. Thread the shrimp onto skewers, 2 or 3 per skewer, place on the hot grill and cook, turning once, until cooked through, 2 to 4 minutes. Or place in a lightly greased pan and broil for 2 to 4 minutes in all, turning once or twice, or roast in the oven for 3 to 5 minutes. Or sauté quickly in the skillet or grill pan for 2 to 4 minutes. Serve the shrimp hot, warm, or at room temperature, with small bowls of Tamarind Sauce on the side.

SERVES 3 TO 4

GRILLED SALMON WITH CHILI-LIME SAUCE

ca nuong gung; nuoc mam chanh

Fine enough for company and fast enough for a weeknight supper, this briefly marinated salmon sparkles with the sharp, sweet, and hot notes of its simple dipping sauce. The same marinade works nicely with other meaty fish, or with shrimp, and the sauce is grand even with plain rice. Toss together a crisp green salad, and you can ring the dinner bell in short order. Or serve it Vietnamese style, with Spinach Sautéed with Garlic and Pepper (page 109), Crab and Asparagus Soup (page 50), and a steaming bowl of rice.

FOR THE SALMON

2 tablespoons vegetable oil

2 tablespoons coarsely chopped fresh ginger

1 tablespoon chopped garlic

1 tablespoon chopped shallots or onion

2 tablespoons fish sauce

1 tablespoon soy sauce

1 tablespoon sugar

1 ¼ pounds thick salmon fillets, or tuna, halibut, or other meaty fish

FOR THE SAUCE

¼ cup fish sauce

3 tablespoons freshly squeezed lime juice or white vinegar

2 tablespoons water

2 tablespoons sugar

¼ teaspoon chili-garlic sauce or other hot sauce

1 tablespoon thinly sliced green onion

To marinate the fish, in a medium bowl, combine the oil, ginger, garlic, shallots, fish sauce, soy sauce, and sugar. Stir to dissolve the sugar and mix everything well. Place the salmon fillets in the bowl and turn to coat with the marinade. Cover and set aside for 20 to 30 minutes, or cover and refrigerate for up to 1 day.

To prepare the sauce, combine all the ingredients in a small bowl. Stir to dissolve the sugar and mix everything well. Place on the serving platter you will use for the fish.

To cook the fish, build a hot charcoal fire, preheat a gas grill, or preheat the oven to 375°F. Place the fish steaks carefully on the grill and grill for about 5 minutes on each side, or until cooked to your liking, or bake for about 15 minutes. Transfer to the serving platter alongside the Chili-Lime Sauce and serve hot or warm.

SERVES 4 TO 6

SALMON STEAKS IN CARAMEL FISH SAUCE

ca kho to

This exceptional dish is a type of *kho*, a traditional clay pot cooking method for braising meat or fish in a sweet-and-salty sauce. You can find clay pots in Asian markets, or simmer your delicious *kho* dish in a small saucepan or small, deep, heavy skillet on your kitchen stove. Any hearty fish steaks will do here. Instead of the salmon, use catfish, mackerel, or bluefish, for example, as long as the steaks fit tightly into the pan so that they are surrounded by the sauce. Like all *kho* dishes, this richly sauced salmon goes wonderfully with a rice-centered meal. Try it with Green Papaya Salad (page 105) or a simple plate of sliced cucumbers and tomatoes for cool contrast. Or serve it with Sweet and Tangy Soup with Pineapple, Tamarind, and Shrimp (page 48). If you use catfish in both this dish and that soup, and serve them with rice, you'll have the classic combination of *com canh chua ca kho to.*

1 tablespoon vegetable oil

1 tablespoon coarsely chopped shallots or onion

1 tablespoon coarsely chopped garlic

¼ cup fish sauce

2 tablespoons sugar

1 tablespoon Caramel Sauce (page 158) **or brown sugar**

⅓ cup water

½ teaspoon black pepper

1¼ pounds salmon steaks or other meaty fish, about 1 inch thick

3 green onions, trimmed, white part chopped, and green part cut into 2-inch lengths

In a small, deep skillet or a small saucepan, combine the oil, shallots, and garlic. Warm over medium-high heat until the garlic sizzles. Add the fish sauce, sugar, Caramel Sauce, water, and pepper and bring to a boil. Cook, stirring now and then, until the sugar dissolves and the sauce thickens a bit, 2 to 3 minutes. Add the salmon steaks and let the sauce return to a gentle boil. Cover and cook for 10 minutes. Carefully turn the steaks over, add the green onions, and cook for 5 minutes more. Transfer the fish steaks to a shallow serving bowl, sauce and all. Serve hot or warm.

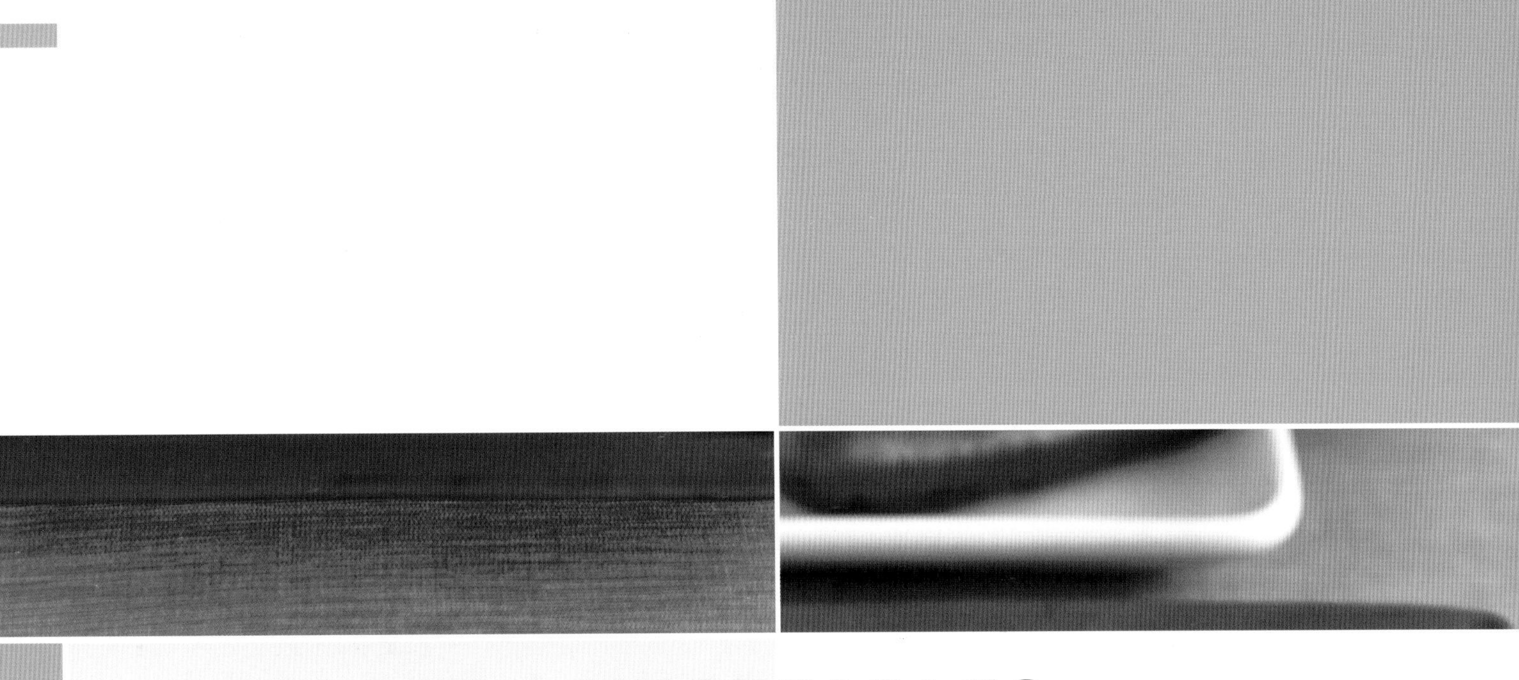

SALADS & VEGETABLES

Although rice anchors a meal throughout Asia, a flotilla of vegetables keeps it company morning, noon, and night, whether sautéed, stirred into soups, pickled, or served raw with a pungent sauce. Asian people eat vegetables often and in quantity, and seldom from a sense of duty or nutritional concerns. They simply like them and prepare them in varied and creative ways; seldom does anyone need coercion to eat her peas. Nowhere in the region, however, are vegetables, salads, and fresh herbs eaten more eagerly and constantly than in Vietnam.

Enormous platters of salad, crudités, and herbs adorn the table at mealtime. Although they create beautiful, glistening green islands on the table, they are neither garnishes nor a still life. Lettuce and herbs allow for folding tidbits of meat or omelet into packets for dipping in a sauce. Cucumbers and bean sprouts refresh the palate between bites of rich, sour, spicy, or salty dishes. They also provide crunch and coolness that contrasts with the soft texture of sustaining rice.

This chapter opens with an everyday pattern for a salad platter, called *dia rau song* in Vietnamese. A base of leaf lettuce is built up with cucumbers, green onions, bean sprouts, chili slices, and a sheaf of aromatic and pungent fresh herb sprigs. *Dia rau song* can be tailored to suit a particular dish, or to feature seasonal goodies along with the basic components. You can pare it down to lettuce cups and cilantro or mint, or build it up with slices of avocado or sweet peppers, chunks of ripe tomato, baby carrots, or sugar snap peas.

Green Papaya Salad (page 105), Roasted Eggplant Salad with Fresh Mint (page 106), and Chopped Watercress Salad with Peanuts (page 112) work beautifully as elements of a traditional Vietnamese meal with rice, but they are also grand as vegetable or salad items on a buffet, or served up with your famous barbecued chicken, baked ziti, or steaks on the grill.

Everyday Pickled Carrots (page 108) and Pickled Bean Sprouts (page 113) are make-ahead condiments you can enjoy with the *dia rau song*, or as accompaniments to anything grilled or saucy. They provide a bright note against the velvet richness of heartier food. Make Everyday Pickled Carrots often, and keep them on hand along with Everyday Dipping Sauce (page 156). You will be able to add the carrots to the sauce, and even better, you will be ready to create Submarine Sandwiches, Saigon Style (page 38) on a moment's notice—the quickest, easiest, most dynamite-delicious recipe in this book.

Cauliflower and spinach round out this collection with two simple stir-fried dishes. Delicious hot, warm, or at room temperature, each illustrates the Vietnamese appreciation for a given vegetable on its own terms. The principle is to do as little as possible, making it easy to appreciate the vegetable's qualities and to cook it often.

SERVES 4

EVERYDAY HERB AND SALAD PLATE

dia rau song

In Vietnam, and everywhere else around the world that Vietnamese people sit down to eat, you will see small plates stacked high with cool green things: leaves of lettuce, bouquets of fresh herbs, slabs of cucumber, stacks of bean sprouts, ovals of fresh hot green chili, and glistening hunks of lime. Watch them disappear as diners pinch, tear, wrap, munch, and dip, eating their way through this petite garden. No stern nutritional guidelines lie behind this tradition, unique on the planet, of enjoying the dance of flavors and textures provided by an abundance of greens and herbs. Vietnamese people devour *dia rau song* because they like to do so, and many dishes presume such a salad plate as an accompaniment. Don't let the number of ingredients overwhelm you. A simple collection of lettuce leaves, cucumbers, and cilantro (or mint or basil) will get you accustomed to the 24/7 Vietnamese salad way.

About 12 cup-shaped tender lettuce leaves, such as Bibb or Boston

1 lime, cut into 6 wedges

2 cups strips or slices of peeled cucumber

2 cups mung bean sprouts

2 green onions, trimmed, cut crosswise into thirds, and then cut lengthwise into shreds

2 fresh jalapeño chilies, cut diagonally into thin ovals

About 1½ cups fresh cilantro, trimmed to 3-inch sprigs

About 1½ cups fresh mint, trimmed to 3-inch sprigs

About 1½ cups fresh basil, trimmed to 3-inch sprigs

Everyday Dipping Sauce (page 156)

Assemble the components of your salad on a big platter, placing lettuce leaves and lime wedges on one end, small piles of cucumber, bean sprouts, green onions, and jalapeño chilies at the other, and the herb sprigs in the center. Divide the Everyday Dipping Sauce into several small bowls so that each guest can easily reach one.

Invite your guests to make small packets for dipping into the sauce. This is done by placing a piece or two of meat or seafood on a lettuce leaf, adding a sprig of herbs, some cucumber, a few bean sprouts, a pinch of green onions, and a slice of chili, and rolling it into a little bundle. The lime wedges are squeezed over soup, noodles, fried rice, or grilled food for a bright, tangy note, while the cucumbers and bean sprouts are enjoyed as a crudité throughout the meal.

To prepare the salad in advance, cover the salad platter loosely with foil, plastic wrap, or a damp kitchen towel and refrigerate for 8 to 12 hours. Set out 30 minutes or so before you plan to serve the accompanying food.

SERVES 4 TO 6

CHICKEN AND CABBAGE SALAD WITH FRESH MINT

goi ga

This simple assembly of everyday ingredients produces a marvelously refreshing dish. The signature Vietnamese herb called *rau ram* is a perfect complement for the chicken and other seasonings, but fresh mint is lovely if you don't have *rau ram.* In Vietnam this salad, *goi ga,* is traditionally served with *mien ga* (page 137), a nourishing chicken dish made with the broth created by poaching chicken for this salad. *Mien* means "noodles," referring to the clear tangle of bean thread noodles that fortify the soup. The *goi ga/mien ga* combination is inspired—a cool, bright-flavored salad paired with a warm, satisfying soupy dish, putting the broth from one to deliciously good use in the other.

1 pound boneless chicken breasts, or 2 cups cooked, shredded chicken

3 tablespoons freshly squeezed lime juice

2 tablespoons fish sauce

1 tablespoon white or cider vinegar, or freshly squeezed lime juice

1 tablespoon sugar

½ teaspoon black pepper

¾ cup very thinly sliced onion

½ cup fresh mint, cilantro, or basil leaves

½ cup *rau ram* leaves (see page 15; optional)

2 cups finely shredded green, savoy, or napa cabbage

¾ cup shredded carrots

3 tablespoons coarsely chopped roasted and salted peanuts (optional)

continued

Put the chicken in a medium saucepan and add 2 to 3 cups of water, enough to cover the chicken by about ½ inch. Bring to a rolling boil over medium-high heat, reduce the heat to maintain a lively simmer, and cook until done, 10 to 15 minutes. Meanwhile, combine the lime juice, fish sauce, vinegar, sugar, and pepper in a medium bowl, and stir to dissolve the sugar and mix everything well. Add the onion and toss to coat. Set aside for 20 to 30 minutes, until you are ready to complete the dish.

Transfer the meat to a plate to cool, reserving the broth for another use, such as making soup or cooking rice. When the chicken is cool, tear it into long, thin shreds. Coarsely chop the mint and the *rau ram,* if you are using it. Add the shredded chicken, cabbage, carrots, mint, and *rau ram* to the bowl of onions and seasonings and toss to coat everything well. Mound the salad on a serving plate and top with chopped peanuts, if you are using them. Serve at room temperature or chilled.

SERVES 4 TO 6

GREEN PAPAYA SALAD

goi du du

Think of this as coleslaw made easier. The hardest part could well be finding a source of green, unripe papaya. Asian markets often carry it. Look for a small one, and expect the green peel to ooze thick, white goo when you cut into it. This is papain, a powerful enzyme used in Southeast Asia as a natural meat tenderizer. To shred up papaya for this salad, halve a papaya, peel and rinse well, seed it, and then grate the sturdy, greenish white flesh on a box grater or in a food processor fitted with the shredding disk. Or look for freshly shredded papaya, ready to use, in the nearest Asian market. I also make this salad with finely shredded cabbage, blanched in boiling water for 1 minute and then refreshed in cold water; or cucumber, thinly sliced and cut in long thin strips; or cooked spaghetti squash; or a mixture of diced green apples and jicama with shredded carrots. Well, you get the idea.

3 tablespoons fish sauce

2 tablespoons freshly squeezed lime juice

2 tablespoons water

2 tablespoons sugar

½ teaspoon chili-garlic sauce

2 ½ cups shredded green papaya, or blanched and refreshed cabbage, shredded cucumber, or cooked spaghetti squash

½ cup shredded carrots

2 tablespoons coarsely chopped fresh mint

2 tablespoons coarsely chopped *rau ram* (see page 15; optional)

3 tablespoons coarsely chopped roasted and salted peanuts

2 tablespoons coarsely chopped fresh cilantro

In a medium bowl, combine the fish sauce, lime juice, water, sugar, and chili-garlic sauce and stir well to make a smooth sauce. Add the green papaya, carrots, mint, and *rau ram,* if using, and toss well. Let stand for 15 minutes. Transfer the salad to a serving platter and top with the chopped peanuts and cilantro. Serve at room temperature.

SERVES 4

ROASTED EGGPLANT SALAD WITH FRESH MINT

ca tim nuong

This humble-looking dish delivers incredibly bright flavor for very little effort. Fancier versions involve topping the salad with sautéed ground pork or chunks of crabmeat. But I prefer this rendition—less work and more reason to appreciate the simple, rustic deliciousness of this dish.

3 slender purple Asian eggplants (about 1 ½ pounds total)

3 tablespoons fish sauce

3 tablespoons freshly squeezed lime juice

2 tablespoons water

2 tablespoons sugar

1 teaspoon minced garlic

1 teaspoon minced fresh hot chilies

1 tablespoon thinly sliced green onion

1 tablespoon coarsely chopped fresh mint

First, roast the eggplants. Prick each one all around with a fork or the tip of a sharp knife to discourage it from bursting as it roasts. Then place the eggplants on a hot grill. Or place an eggplant right on the burner of a gas or electric stove, over low to medium-low heat. Turn the eggplant as it browns and puffs, roasting it as evenly as possible, until it is fairly soft and blistery brown, 3 to 5 minutes. Transfer to a plate to cool, and cook the remaining ones the same way.

When the eggplants are cool enough to touch, peel them gently, holding them under cool running water, when necessary, to get the job done. You can leave them whole with the stem attached, or discard the stem and chop the eggplants into big pieces. Place the eggplants in a small, shallow serving bowl and set aside.

Prepare the sauce, combining the fish sauce, lime juice, water, and sugar in a medium bowl. Stir well to dissolve the sugar. Stir in the garlic and chilies, and then pour this sauce over the eggplant. Scatter the green onion and mint over the dressed eggplant and serve at room temperature.

EVERYDAY PICKLED CARROTS

ca cai ca rot chua

This tasty carrot relish should live in your refrigerator, along with two bunches of fresh cilantro and a handful of fresh jalapeño chilies, so that you are never more than a baguette's length away from enjoying Vietnam's signature sub sandwich, *Banh Mi* (page 38). The carrots are wonderful in Everyday Dipping Sauce (page 156) as an edible garnish, and they make a tasty addition to noodle soups and Big, Cool Noodle Bowls (page 133). Substitute shredded white daikon radish for half the carrots if you like, for a beautiful contrast in color and texture. I shred carrots on a box grater or in the food processor if I have time, and I use already shredded carrots from the produce section if I'm in a rush.

1½ cups water

¾ cup white vinegar

¾ cup sugar

1 teaspoon salt

3 cups shredded carrots (about ¾ pound)**, or 1½ cups shredded carrots and 1½ cups shredded daikon**

Combine the water, vinegar, sugar, and salt in a small saucepan and place over medium heat. Cook for 3 to 4 minutes, swirling once or twice, until the sugar and salt dissolve and the sauce is clear and smooth. Transfer to a bowl and cool to room temperature. (Pour the brine into a cake pan, pie pan, or a metal bowl and place it in the freezer briefly if you're in a hurry.)

Add the shredded carrots to the cooled brine, toss well, and set aside for 20 to 30 minutes. Serve at room temperature, or transfer to a jar, cover, and refrigerate until serving time. Scoop out carrots from the brine as you need them and store the remainder in the refrigerator for up to 5 days.

SERVES 4

SPINACH SAUTÉED WITH GARLIC AND PEPPER

rau muong xao toi

Elsewhere in Southeast Asia, cooks tend to fortify stir-fried vegetables with a handful of meat. In the Vietnamese kitchen, vegetables often make a solo appearance, cooked simply to enhance their natural appeal. Such vegetable dishes are usually enjoyed with lots of rice and other dishes featuring meat or fish. Each dish has its own distinct flavor, and they are delicious eaten together or separately.

2 tablespoons vegetable oil

1 tablespoon coarsely chopped garlic

8 to 10 cups fresh spinach leaves
(about 1 ¼ pounds)

2 tablespoons fish sauce

½ teaspoon black pepper

¼ cup water

In a large, heavy skillet or a wok, combine the oil and garlic and cook over medium-high heat until the garlic sizzles and releases its aroma. Add the spinach and cook for 1 minute. Gently turn the pile of spinach to expose all the leaves to the heat. Add the fish sauce, pepper, and water, toss well, and then cook, turning often, until the spinach is wilted and tender, 1 to 2 minutes. Transfer to a deep platter, sauce and all, and serve hot, warm, or at room temperature.

SERVES 4

CAULIFLOWER WITH GARLIC AND PEPPER

bong cai xao

Cook the cauliflower until it's tender and nicely seasoned but still in possession of a little crunch. You could add a splash of sesame oil just before that last toss for a delicious variation, or try cooking broccoli florets the same way. This is usually served hot with rice, soup, and other dishes, but I also like it at room temperature or cold if I have any left over.

2 tablespoons vegetable oil

1 tablespoon chopped garlic

About 4 cups small cauliflower florets

2 tablespoons fish sauce

2 tablespoons water

1 teaspoon sugar

½ teaspoon black pepper

2 green onions, trimmed and cut into 1-inch lengths

2 tablespoons coarsely chopped fresh cilantro, dill, or mint

Heat the oil in a large skillet over medium-high heat until a bit of garlic sizzles at once, and then add the garlic. Toss well and add the cauliflower. Cook for 1 minute, and then toss well, exposing the other sides to the hot pan. Add the fish sauce, water, sugar, pepper, and green onions and cook, tossing often, until the cauliflower is tender but still pleasantly crunchy, about 2 minutes. Stir in the cilantro, toss once more, and transfer to a serving plate deep enough to hold the sauce, or to a shallow bowl. Serve hot or warm.

SERVES 4 TO 6

CHOPPED WATERCRESS SALAD WITH PEANUTS

tron sa lach son

You can use baby spinach leaves, a mix of spinach and arugula, or thinly sliced celery, or cucumber sliced or chopped, for this refreshing salad.

2 bunches watercress

¼ cup white vinegar or apple cider vinegar

2 tablespoons water

2 tablespoons sugar

1 tablespoon vegetable oil

½ teaspoon salt

¼ teaspoon black pepper

3 tablespoons coarsely chopped dry-roasted salted peanuts

Separate watercress, trim away coarse ends, rinse in cold water and drain well. Chop into 2-inch lengths. Measure out 3 cups watercress, reserving remaining greens for another use. In a small bowl combine the vinegar, water, sugar, oil, salt, and pepper, and stir well to dissolve sugar and salt. Pour over watercress and toss well. Transfer seasoned watercress to a small platter, sprinkle with chopped peanuts, and serve.

PICKLED BEAN SPROUTS

These simple preserved bean sprouts serve as a tangy and salty counterpoint to rich, sweet dishes, such as fish, shrimp, or pork simmered in a clay pot, and Pork and Hard-Boiled Eggs Simmered in Coconut Juice (page 81).

3 cups water

¼ cup white or cider vinegar

1 tablespoon salt

1 teaspoon sugar

3 cups mung bean sprouts

Bring the water, vinegar, salt, and sugar to a boil over medium-hight heat in a medium saucepan and stir to dissolve the salt and sugar. Set aside to cool to room temperature. Meanwhile, pour the sprouts into a medium bowl and add water to cover. Discard any green mung bean hulls and tired sprouts you find, drain well, and set aside.

When the brine is cool, pour it over the bean sprouts and set aside for at least 1 hour. Serve at room temperature, or cover and refrigerate for up to 3 days. To serve, scoop sprouts out of the brine and transfer to a small serving bowl or plate.

RICE

Two assumptions underlie most home-cooked Vietnamese meals. One is that you will include generous amounts of *nuoc cham* (Everyday Dipping Sauce, page 156) to flavor your meal. The other is that you will eat the substantial dishes with lots of plain, wonderful, unseasoned rice. Saucy *kho* dishes simmered in a clay pot presume this, as do Sweet and Tangy Soup with Pineapple, Tamarind, and Shrimp (page 48), or *canh chua tom*, and Lemongrass Chicken (page 54), *ga xao xa ot*.

Exceptions abound, given the Vietnamese genius with noodles, but rice gives Vietnamese cooking its full glory, and you will probably want to include it often as you enjoy cooking the recipes in this book.

On page 116, you will find a recipe for Everyday Rice, which you can cook first thing and then set on the back burner, literally, to finish cooking on its own while you put the rest of the meal together. If you eat rice often, as I do, you may want to consider an electric rice cooker, which makes the job quite simple, and gives excellent results.

Shrimp Fried Rice (page 122) is worth putting in your repertoire ASAP. It takes the place of a sandwich in the Asian home kitchen, a speedy, satisfying something to eat made with whatever happens to be in the fridge. It involves a little more action than sandwich making (heating the pot and chopping a green onion or a piece of cold cooked chicken), but not much.

Sticky Rice (page 117) is an amazing ingredient. It requires a little extra attention, since it needs 3 hours or more of soaking in advance, and a means of steaming it to bring it to its tender, nourishing, and fun-to-eat state. In Laos, and in the northern and northeastern regions of Thailand, plain, long-grain sticky rice is the daily bread, but in Vietnam it is a much-loved option, often eaten as a breakfast on the run or between-meals snack, topped with various simple, incredibly delicious toppings, including peanuts, toasted sesame seeds, coconut shreds, sugar, and salt.

Often enjoyed with roasted and grilled meat, sticky rice is a mainstay of vegetarian cooking, a significant genre within Vietnamese cuisine. I adore sticky rice, and hope you will try it and enjoy it as well. If you do, consider getting a cone-shaped steaming set (see page 22), designed for the job of steaming soaked sticky rice. It's an inexpensive, charming traditional country cooking implement that is still viable in the kitchens of the third millennium. The simple way in which it does its job more than compensates for the need to find a spot for one more thing in your kitchen.

This chapter concludes with Soothing Rice Porridge with Salmon and Fresh Dill (page 125) and Hearty Chicken and Rice Porridge with Fresh Ginger (page 124). These two versions of Asian-style rice porridge make hearty one-bowl meals. They need a little time to simmer, but the assembly of each porridge is quite simple, and the resulting dish is a comfort-food feast.

SERVES 4; MAKES 4 TO 5 CUPS OF COOKED RICE

EVERYDAY RICE

com

While I count on an electric rice cooker as a mainstay of my kitchen, I like knowing how to cook rice in a pot on top of the stove. That way I'm ready even if the power goes off (we have a gas stove), or if I'm on a camping trip, or if I want to cook a Vietnamese feast at someone else's home. Get good at it, and then keep doing it until you have the recipe in your head and hands.

1 ½ cups long-grain rice

2 cups water

Measure the rice into a medium saucepan and add cold water to cover the grains. Swirl the grains with your hand, drain well, and then add the measured 2 cups of water. Bring to a gentle boil, uncovered, over medium heat. Let the rice continue to boil gently until the water level drops below the level of the rice so that it looks dry. Stir well, cover, and reduce the heat to low. Cook for 15 minutes, remove from the heat, and then let stand, covered, for 10 minutes more. Fluff gently with a fork and serve hot or warm.

STICKY RICE

xôi

Look for long-grain sticky rice in Asian markets. Most packages label it "glutinous rice" or "sweet rice," even though it contains no gluten and is not sweet unless you add sugar to it. Plan ahead to make sticky rice, because it needs to soak for at least 3 hours in order to steam properly. The ideal kitchen tool for steaming sticky rice is a Laotian-style cone-shaped woven basket, which nests in a deep metal pot containing boiling water. The basket of soaked rice sits directly over the flow of steam, allowing the rice to cook evenly and fast. You can buy this two-part steamer set in many Asian markets, or see Mail-Order Sources (page 162). You could also use large bamboo steamer trays, designed to fit over several inches of water in a wok. A third option is a big metal steaming set, which has several trays, through which steam can flow. It takes up some storage space, but it has multiple uses as a steaming vessel, unlike the cone-shaped basket setup, which works only for sticky rice.

1 ½ cups long-grain sticky rice

Water for soaking and steaming

Put the raw sticky rice into a medium bowl and add enough water to cover it by 2 inches. Leave it to soak for at least 3 hours or overnight. Set out your steaming vessel (see the description above).

To cook the rice, bring 4 to 6 inches of water to a vigorous boil over medium heat in the base of your steamer. If you are using a Laotian-style steamer, drain the rice well and transfer it to the cone-shaped steaming basket. Set the basket of rice grains securely over the boiling water, cover with a folded kitchen towel or a metal lid, and let the rice cook in a steady flow of steam until it plumps up, glistens, and changes color from bright white to translucent ivory, 20 to 30 minutes. To use the bamboo or metal trays, line the tray with a kitchen towel, cheesecloth, or a banana leaf, and spread the soaked and drained sticky rice over it in a

■ *continued*

fairly even layer. Or steam the rice in a shallow, heat-proof bowl placed directly on the tray. When the time is up, test the rice by scooping up a small mouthful, rolling it into a ball, and eating it. If it is tender and pleasantly chewy, the rice is ready.

Turn out the cooked sticky rice onto a cutting board or tray and quickly spread it out into a fairly even layer. Let it cool and release steam for 5 to 10 minutes. Then gather the warm rice into a large clump and transfer it to a serving plate or a covered serving basket. To keep it for more than 30 minutes before serving, cover it with a kitchen towel or place in a tightly closed container to help keep it moist. Serve hot, warm, or at room temperature. To reheat cooked sticky rice, sprinkle with water and heat gently in the steamer or in a microwave just until softened and warm.

SERVES 4

BLACK STICKY RICE

xoi nep

In Vietnam, black sticky rice is enjoyed at breakfast or lunch, as well as in Black Sticky Rice Pudding (page 144), a sweet treat. *Xoi nep* is a form of brown rice with a dense, chewy texture. It needs a little longer cooking time than polished white rice. High in amylopectin, the starch that causes rice grains to cling together, it can be soaked and steamed like white, milled Sticky Rice (page 117). Serve this with chopsticks or a fork as the centerpiece of a rice meal, or season it with butter and salt and enjoy it as a side dish with grilled or roasted food. For breakfast we like it with a topping of brown sugar, toasted sweetened shredded coconut, and chopped roasted and salted peanuts or walnuts.

1 ½ cups black sticky rice

3 cups water

In a medium saucepan with a tight-fitting lid, rinse the rice and drain it well. Add the 3 cups of water and bring to a lively boil over medium-high heat. Stir well and cook for 10 minutes. Stir well again and reduce the heat to medium, maintaining a lively simmer. Cook, stirring well now and then, until the rice is plump, shiny, and tender with a soft, nutty crunch, about 25 minutes. It should be fairly dry. Reduce the heat to low and cook for 3 minutes more, stirring and scraping once or twice. Remove from the heat, transfer to a serving bowl, and serve hot or warm.

SERVES 4; MAKES ABOUT 3 CUPS OF STICKY RICE

STICKY RICE WITH MUNG BEANS, NORTHERN STYLE

xoi dau xanh

The tiny, oval, yellow centers of mung beans are beloved in Vietnamese cuisine. Often used in sweets and in steamed foods wrapped in banana leaf packets, they are also cooked with sticky rice in various ways. In northern Vietnam, mung bean centers are soaked and steamed along with sticky rice, giving the rice a lovely golden color while increasing its nutritional value. Southern versions of sticky rice with mung beans usually include coconut milk and sugar, taking the dish in a sweeter direction. The topping is extraordinarily delicious—doubly crunchy and pleasingly salty and sweet. You can enjoy this as a snack, or as a rice dish to enjoy along with grilled meats and fish.

FOR THE STICKY RICE

¾ cup long-grain sticky rice

¼ cup yellow mung bean centers

Water for soaking and steaming

½ teaspoon vegetable oil

¼ teaspoon salt

TOPPING (OPTIONAL)

3 tablespoons white sesame seeds, toasted (see page 20)

⅓ cup coarsely chopped roasted and salted peanuts

2 tablespoons sugar

At least 3 hours before you plan to serve, combine the raw sticky rice and the mung bean centers in a medium bowl. Add water to cover them, swirl with your hands, and drain well. Repeat the process, rinsing away most of the yellow color released by the beans. Add fresh water to cover by about 1 inch, and set aside to soak for at least 3 hours and up to 12 hours.

To cook the rice and beans, drain them well, and then mix in the oil and salt. Scrape the mixture into the basket or onto the cloth-lined tray of your steaming vessel (see page 117), and place it over a steamer base filled with 4 to 6 inches of water. Bring the water to a rolling boil over high heat, and then adjust the heat to maintain an active flow of steam.

When steam is flowing through the rice and beans, cover with a folded kitchen towel, a big square of banana leaf, or a lid, and let it steam until the tiny yellow beans are tender and the rice plumps up, changing from bright white to a warm ivory shade, 20 to 35 minutes. The rice should be tender to the bite. It should stick to itself when rolled into a little ball, but not stick to your fingers.

While the rice and beans steam, prepare the topping, if using. You can chop the toasted sesame seeds, pound them lightly with a mortar and pestle, or leave them whole. Combine the peanuts, sesame seeds, and sugar in a small bowl, stirring to mix them well. Place on the serving platter you will use for the rice and beans.

Turn out the cooked sticky rice and beans onto a cutting board or tray and quickly spread them out into a fairly even layer. Let cool and release steam for 5 to 10 minutes.

Gather the warm rice and beans into a large clump and transfer to the serving platter with the bowl of topping, if using. Sprinkle the topping over the rice and serve hot, warm, or at room temperature.

SERVES 4

SHRIMP FRIED RICE

com chien

Throughout Asia, fried rice is a standard dish, and the Vietnamese version is a delicious, endlessly variable ticket to quick and easy feasts. This recipe is a little bit fancy because it includes an egg pancake that is cooked ahead and shredded. You can leave out the egg, or push the rice away from the center and scramble the egg right in the middle of the pan toward the end of the cooking time. You can also use chopped cooked chicken or ham instead of the shrimp, adding either meat to the pan along with the rice since they are already cooked. I add frozen peas or edamame beans when I want fried rice to be a one-plate supper. For a vegetarian version, omit the fish sauce and shrimp, increase the salt to 1½ teaspoons, and add pineapple, cashews, and frozen peas.

4 cups cold, cooked rice (page 116), **preferably chilled**

2 tablespoons vegetable oil

1 egg, well beaten

1 tablespoon coarsely chopped garlic

½ cup coarsely chopped onion

12 medium shrimp, peeled and deveined

2 tablespoons fish sauce

½ teaspoon salt

¼ teaspoon black pepper

3 tablespoons coarsely chopped green onion

Crumble the rice with your fingers to break up any big lumps, and place a serving platter and a table knife by the stove. Heat a large, deep skillet or a wok over medium-high heat. Add about 2 teaspoons of the oil and swirl to coat the pan lightly. Add the beaten egg and tilt the pan to make a thin egg pancake. Cook until set, about 1 minute, and then turn it out onto the serving platter.

Add the remaining oil to the pan, along with the garlic and onion, and cook until sizzling and fragrant, 1 to 2 minutes. Scatter the shrimp in the pan and cook, tossing once or twice, until they are pink, 1 to 2 minutes. Add the rice and cook, tossing now and then, until shiny and heated through, 3 to 5 minutes.

Meanwhile, roll up the egg pancake into a cylinder, cut it crosswise into thin ribbons with the table knife, and keep them handy on the platter near the stove. Add the fish sauce, salt, pepper, and green onion to the rice and toss. Add the egg ribbons, and cook, tossing well, for 1 more minute. Mound the fried rice on a serving platter and serve hot or warm.

SERVES 4 TO 6

HEARTY CHICKEN AND RICE PORRIDGE WITH FRESH GINGER

chao ga

Comfort food isn't always this easy to make, nor this tasty. *Chao ga* is hearty enough for supper and simple enough to fix on the busiest day. If you have time, add a little extra flavor by first frying the rice grains and a little chopped onion in a tablespoon or two of oil, until the onion is fragrant and the rice grains turn bright white. Add them to the boiling stock and simmer until soft. Serve *chao ga* with a bowl of either Everyday Dipping Sauce (page 156) or Ginger-Lime Dipping Sauce (page 157) on the side.

3 cups chicken broth

3 cups water

½ pound boneless chicken breasts or thighs

½ cup long-grain rice, rinsed and drained

1 tablespoon finely chopped fresh ginger

1 tablespoon fish sauce

1 teaspoon black pepper

2 tablespoons thinly sliced green onion

1 tablespoon chopped fresh cilantro

Combine the broth and water in a medium saucepan and bring to a rolling boil over high heat. Add the chicken, lower the heat to maintain a lively simmer, and cook until the chicken is done, about 10 minutes. Transfer to a plate to cool, and return the broth to a boil.

Stir in the rice and ginger, and lower the heat to maintain a gentle simmer. Cook the rice until soft, 25 minutes. Meanwhile, pull apart or cut the cooled chicken into shreds and set aside. When the rice is tender, add the shredded chicken, fish sauce, pepper, green onion, and cilantro, and stir well. Remove the porridge from the heat and serve hot.

SOOTHING RICE PORRIDGE WITH SALMON AND FRESH DILL

chao ca

Serve this deluxe version of humble rice porridge with a saucer of sliced cucumbers and a bowl of steamed broccoli, seasoned with a splash of Asian sesame oil and a little salt. You can try *chao ca* with catfish, halibut, snapper, or another firm-fleshed fish, but the salmon does add beautiful color. If you have *chao ca* left over, expect it to thicken up a good bit once it cools off. To reheat it you can add a cup or two of chicken broth to return it to its original texture, or simply enjoy it in its new substantial state, adding a little salt, a few herbs, or a splash of lime as needed, to refresh the soup.

3 cups water

3 cups chicken broth

½ cup long-grain rice, rinsed and drained

½ pound salmon fillets, or catfish, tilapia, or other firm-fleshed fish

2 tablespoons fish sauce

½ teaspoon black pepper

2 tablespoons thinly sliced green onion

2 tablespoons coarsely chopped fresh cilantro

2 tablespoons coarsely chopped fresh dill

Combine the water and broth in a medium saucepan and bring to a rolling boil over high heat. Stir in the rice and lower the heat to maintain a gentle simmer. Cook until the rice is soft, 25 minutes. Meanwhile, cut the fish crosswise into 2-inch lengths, and then cut each piece into generous chunks.

When the rice is tender, add the fish and let the soup return to a gentle boil. Cook until the fish is done, 2 to 3 minutes. Add the fish sauce, pepper, and green onion and stir well. Remove from the heat and stir in the cilantro and dill. Serve hot or warm.

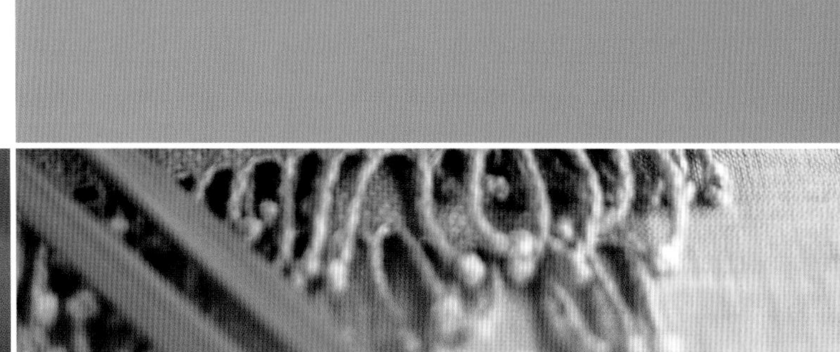

NOODLES

Asian noodle dishes have ancient roots in the cuisines of China, but nobody has cultivated, nourished, and brought them to full flower like the people of Vietnam. Not only do they cook up spectacular renditions of the standard noodle repertoire (in soup, sautéed, and in a bowl dressed with a few tasty condiments and herbs); they have also created a repertoire of superb noodle dishes unique to Vietnamese cuisine.

Many of these noodle feasts are beyond the scope of a quick-and-easy book, requiring multiple ingredients and extensive preparation methods. These dishes are seldom prepared at home, even in Vietnam, because of the effort involved. But many Vietnamese noodle dishes are far simpler, and this chapter contains a half dozen recipes you will love.

First come two soupy noodle classics. *Pho* Noodles with Beef, Hanoi Style (page 128), the legendary dish of northern Vietnam, and *Hu Tieu* Noodles with Pork and Shrimp, Saigon Style (page 131), are dishes you can easily create at home, especially if you invite a few helpers to set out bowls, chop up herbs, and keep you company as you put the dish together.

Big, Cool Noodle Bowl (page 133) illustrates Vietnam's culinary genius in devising new ways to put familiar ingredients together. It is a type of *bun,* a dish in which thin rice noodles are piled into a big bowl over a small bed of salad greens, and then topped with hearty treats, such as grilled beef, pork meatballs, lemongrass shrimp, or even Vietnam's crispy signature spring rolls, *cha gio.* It is finished with a carnival of toppings, from chopped peanuts and cilantro to cucumbers and Everyday Dipping Sauce (page 156).

Rice noodles are easily stir-fried if you know a few guidelines. Once you have learned them, you can vary the components of the recipe for *hu tieu xao,* or Rice Noodles Stir-Fried with Pork and Shrimp (page 134), to your liking. Bean thread noodles are the simplest noodles of all to work with. They are shelf stable, quick cooking, eager to absorb other flavors, and inexplicably pleasing to eat. Two recipes showcase them: One is *mien xao tom,* or Bean Thread Noodles Stir-Fried with Shrimp (page 138). The other is *mien ga,* or Bean Thread Noodles with Chicken (page 137), a classic dish traditionally served with *goi ga,* or Chicken and Cabbage Salad with Fresh Mint (page 102).

SERVES 4

PHO NOODLES WITH BEEF, HANOI STYLE

pho bo

Consider *pho,* a small word for a big bowl of noodles in soup. The soup is clear, delicate, and redolent of cinnamon, star anise, and ginger. The noodles swirl just below the surface of the steaming broth, barely visible beneath slices of beef, slivers of onion, and a tumble of crisp bean sprouts. A miniscule mountain of aromatic herbs, big green slices of chili, and a chunk of lime attend the bowl, for seasoning everything just so. *Pho* gives nourishment and pleasure to anyone who sits down to enjoy a bowl. For Vietnamese people far from home, eating *pho* can set things right, restore the spirit, touch the heart. *Pho* is a small word for a big, steaming, herb-laden bowl of comfort food.

This recipe provides a blueprint for a streamlined home version of *pho.* It involves a few steps, but none of them is difficult, and with good company and several pairs of hands, everything can be ready in under an hour. *Pho* takes a little more time than some dishes, but it gives you a memorable, delicious reward.

FOR THE BROTH

8 cups chicken broth

1 pound round steak, sliced crosswise into 1-inch strips

3 cinnamon sticks

3 whole cloves

3 star anise

1 unpeeled medium onion, quartered lengthwise

½ cup peeled and very coarsely chopped fresh ginger

½ pound linguine-width dried rice noodles, often labeled *banh pho*

2 tablespoons fish sauce

1 teaspoon sugar

½ teaspoon salt

3 cups bean sprouts

1 cup very thinly sliced onion or shallots

1 cup coarsely chopped fresh Asian basil, cilantro, or mint, or a combination

½ cup thinly sliced green onion

¼ cup freshly squeezed lime juice

2 fresh jalapeño chilies, cut diagonally into thin ovals

1 ¼ pounds boneless rib-eye, strip, or flank steak

continued

To prepare the broth, combine the chicken broth, sliced round steak, cinnamon sticks, cloves, and star anise in a stockpot or a very large saucepan. Bring to a gentle boil over medium-high heat.

Meanwhile, brown the onion and ginger to bring out their flavor: heat a large skillet over medium-high heat until very hot, about 1 minute. Add the quartered onion and ginger and let them cook on one surface until handsomely browned but not burnt. Turn and sear the other surface, and continue cooking until all the pieces are well browned and fragrant. Add the charred onion and ginger to the stockpot, and let everything boil gently for 1 hour.

While the broth is cooking, soften the rice noodles by immersing them in a medium bowl of warm water until they become flexible and bright white, 15 to 20 minutes. Drain well and set aside.

Remove the broth from the heat, and stir in the fish sauce, sugar, and salt. Strain the broth into a large saucepan, discarding all the solids. Or, if you are preparing your *pho* in advance, strain the broth into a storage container instead. Let it cool to room temperature, cover, and refrigerate for up to 2 days.

About 30 minutes before you plan to serve the dish, prepare the noodles, boneless beef, and accompaniments. Place the bean sprouts, sliced onion, fresh herbs, green onion, lime juice, and chilies near 4 big Asian-style noodle bowls, pasta plates, or soup bowls in which you will serve the broth. Bring a large saucepan of water to a rolling boil over high heat for the noodles. Meanwhile, pour the broth into a saucepan, bring it to a gentle boil over medium-high heat, and adjust the heat to maintain a lively simmer. Cut the steak in half crosswise, put both pieces in the simmering broth, and cook for 10 minutes, or until medium-rare. Transfer the steak to a cutting board, slice into thin, bite-sized strips, and set aside.

Shortly before serving, cook the noodles: Drop the softened rice noodles into the boiling water, remove from the heat, and let stand for 10 minutes, stirring once or twice to separate any noodle clumps into strands. Meanwhile, bring the simmering broth to a rolling boil.

Drain the noodles well, and quickly divide them up among the 4 bowls (about 1 cup per bowl). Top each noodle bowl with one-fourth of the sliced steak, bean sprouts, onion, herbs, green onion, lime juice, and chilies. Ladle hot broth (about 1½ cups) over the noodles in each bowl, and serve at once. Be sure to provide each guest with a fork or chopsticks, and an Asian soup spoon or a large spoon.

SERVES 4

HU TIEU NOODLES WITH PORK AND SHRIMP, SAIGON STYLE

hu tieu saigon

Hu tieu is a bright bowl of rice noodles in soup, enjoyed from dawn to midnight throughout the Mekong Delta (see recipe photograph on page 8). Noodle shops and itinerant noodle vendors do good business near fresh markets, schools, bus stations, and ferry landings, wherever people congregate for commerce, company, or en route from here to there. *Hu tieu* starts with a broth of chicken and pork, often fortified with an infusion of dried squid and dried shrimp. Atop a mound of slender rice noodles, *hu tieu* vendors compose a colorful design: pink shrimp, thin slices of barbecued pork, thinly sliced celery, fresh bean sprouts, sprinklings of cilantro leaves, green onions, and thinly sliced chilies, a shower of chopped peanuts and fried shallots, and a squeeze of lime. For fried shallots, fry thinly sliced shallots in hot oil until nicely browned, drain well and set aside to cool. *Hu tieu* is sometimes served as a dry noodle bowl, with garnishes atop the hot rice noodles and a small steaming bowl of the broth presented on the side.

FOR THE NOODLES AND SOUP

½ pound dried rice noodles, preferably the linguine-width *banh pho*, or angel hair pasta

5 cups chicken broth

1 tablespoon fish sauce

2 thick bone-in pork chops (about 1 ¼ pounds)**, or 1 pound boneless pork, or 1 pound barbecued or roast pork**

½ pound medium shrimp, peeled and deveined

ACCOMPANIMENTS

2 cups bean sprouts

3 stalks celery, trimmed and cut diagonally into thin slices (about 1 cup)

½ cup thinly sliced green onion

½ cup coarsely chopped fresh cilantro

½ cup coarsely chopped roasted and salted peanuts

¼ cup freshly squeezed lime juice

2 fresh jalapeño chilies, cut diagonally into thin ovals

continued

To prepare the noodles and soup, soften the rice noodles in warm water to cover for about 15 minutes. Meanwhile, bring the broth and fish sauce to a gentle boil in a large saucepan over medium-high heat. Cut most of the meat off the pork chop bones, and then add both the meaty bones and meat to the broth. Reduce the heat to maintain a lively simmer, and cook the pork for 10 minutes, skimming off any foam that rises to the top. (If using barbecued or roast pork, slice thinly, add to the stock, and simmer for 2 to 3 minutes.)

While the soup cooks, bring another large pot of water to a rolling boil over high heat. Drain the softened noodles, add them to the pot, and remove from the heat at once. Let stand for 10 minutes, stirring now and then to pull apart any clumps. Drain well and set aside.

Remove the meat from the simmering broth, leaving the bones in, and set the meat aside to cool. Add the shrimp to the broth and cook until they are bright pink, firm, and cooked through, 2 to 3 minutes. Remove at once and set aside with the cooked meat. Cut the meat into thin strips, and cut the shrimp in half lengthwise.

To serve the noodles, place 4 big Asian-style noodle bowls or pasta plates or regular soup bowls near the stove, along with all the accompaniments. Bring the broth to a rolling boil over high heat. Divide the noodles among the bowls, and then place one-fourth of the remaining ingredients on top of the noodles in each bowl: slices of pork, several shrimp halves, with the pink side up, bean sprouts, celery, green onion, cilantro, peanuts, fried shallots (if using), lime juice, and chilies. Ladle about 1 ½ cups of hot broth over each bowl of noodles and serve at once, providing each diner with a fork or chopsticks, and an Asian soup spoon or a large spoon.

SERVES 4

BIG, COOL NOODLE BOWL WITH ROAST CHICKEN, CUCUMBERS, AND FRESH MINT

bun ga nuong

This is the pattern for endless delicious meals based upon the winning formula of *bun:* a pile of soft rice noodles, a serving of flavorful roast or grilled meat, a refreshing array of greens and herbs, and a generous splash of Vietnam's incomparably delicious theme sauce, *nuoc cham* (Everyday Dipping Sauce, page 156). My favorite version is anything I can compose using ready-to-savor ingredients, such as chunks of roast chicken from the deli, slices of barbecued pork *(char siu)* or roast duck from Chinatown, or slices of grilled flank steak from yesterday's barbecue. If I'm planning a Big, Cool Noodle Bowl meal from scratch, rather than assembling one on short order, I make up a quick batch of Lemongrass Beef (page 68).

½ pound thin dried rice noodles or angel hair pasta

2 cups shredded lettuce or spring salad mix

3 cups shredded roast chicken, or ½ pound grilled shrimp, or ½ recipe Lemongrass Beef (page 68)

2 cups peeled and sliced cucumber

1 cup small sprigs of fresh mint and fresh cilantro combined

2 cups mung bean sprouts (optional)

1 cup Everyday Pickled Carrots (page 108) **or shredded carrots** (optional)

⅓ cup thinly sliced green onion

¾ cup chopped roasted and salted peanuts

Double recipe Everyday Dipping Sauce (page 156; about 1 cup)

To cook the rice noodles, bring a large saucepan, Dutch oven, or pasta pot of water to a rolling boil over high heat. Drop in the noodles, remove from the heat, and let stand for 10 minutes, using tongs or a slotted spoon and a fork to separate the noodles and let them cook evenly. When the noodles are tender, drain, rinse in cold water, and drain again. You'll have about 6 cups of cooked noodles. Let stand while you prepare the remaining ingredients.

Set out 4 big Asian-style noodle bowls or pasta plates or soup bowls. Divide the ingredients evenly among the bowls: lettuce first, topped with 1½ cups of noodles in each bowl. Put the roast chicken on one side, and the cucumber, fresh herbs, and any optional ingredients you're using on the other. Sprinkle green onions and peanuts over the chicken, pour ¼ cup of Everyday Dipping Sauce over each portion of the noodles, and serve at once, inviting your guests to toss everything together as they begin to eat.

SERVES 2 TO 4

RICE NOODLES STIR-FRIED WITH PORK AND SHRIMP

hu tieu xao

You, too, can cook a fabulous platter of stir-fried rice noodles right in your own kitchen if you follow a few simple rules. First, prepare the dried rice noodles so that they will soften and season themselves with just a few turns in the hot pan. Second, set everything you'll need right by the stove, measured out and ready to cook. Third, have a serving platter and any guests handy, because hot-out-of-the pan noodles are a true Asian treat. Once you've cooked this a time or two, you'll know how to create noodle feasts galore based on what you like and have handy. Leave out the pork, or toss in mushrooms, zucchini, or shredded carrots. Scramble an egg into the pan near the end of cooking, add a spoonful of chopped fresh chilies or hot sauce, or finish the dish with cilantro, chopped peanuts, and a squeeze of lime. It may never be quite as easy for you as making a sandwich, but it might be close. Wide rice noodles are the typical choice, but use any width of fresh or softened rice noodle, Chinese egg noodles, or any cooked pasta.

¼ pound fettuccine- or linguine-width dried rice noodles

6 green onions, trimmed, white part coarsely chopped, and green tops cut into 2-inch lengths

2 tablespoons fish sauce

2 tablespoons water

2 tablespoons soy sauce

½ teaspoon sugar

½ teaspoon salt

½ teaspoon black pepper

2 tablespoons vegetable oil

1 tablespoon chopped garlic

¼ pound boneless pork, cut against the grain into thin, 2-inch strips, or Chinese-style roast pork or roast duck

12 medium shrimp, peeled and deveined

2 ½ cups fresh spinach leaves

1 cup mung bean sprouts (optional)

■ *continued*

Soften the rice noodles in warm water to cover until they become flexible and bright white, 15 to 20 minutes. Bring a large pot of water to a rolling boil over high heat. Drain the softened noodles, add them to the pot, and remove from the heat. Let stand for 6 to 8 minutes. Drain well and put in a bowl by the stove. You will have about 2 ½ cups of noodles.

In a small bowl, combine the green onion tops, fish sauce, water, soy sauce, sugar, salt, and pepper, and stir well to dissolve the sugar and salt. Place by the stove, along with tongs or a big spatula for moving the noodles around, all the remaining ingredients.

In a large, deep skillet or a wok, heat the oil over medium-high heat for 30 seconds. Add the garlic and the white portion of the green onions and toss well. Add the pork and cook just until it changes color, about 1 minute. Add the fish sauce mixture, toss well, and then add the noodles. Cook for 1 minute or so, tossing and pushing the noodles to season and heat them evenly, then push them to one side and add the shrimp.

Cook the shrimp on one side until pink. Toss to let the other side cook, and then add the spinach and bean sprouts (if using). Gently scoop up the mass of noodles to cover the shrimp and vegetables, and let them cook for 30 seconds. Toss everything well, adding up to ¼ cup water if the pan is getting dry. Check to see that the pork and shrimp are cooked through, and transfer the noodles to a serving platter. Pull a few shrimp to the top and serve at once.

BEAN THREAD NOODLES WITH CHICKEN

mien ga

This classic dish is very simple, very fast, and very good. *Ga* means "chicken" and *mien* means "bean thread noodles." Traditionally it is served with *goi ga,* Chicken and Cabbage Salad with Fresh Mint (page 102). Poaching chicken for the salad creates a tasty broth, perfect for simmering bean thread noodles and a handful of fresh herbs to make this dish. I like to cut the bean thread noodles down to a manageable size after softening and before cooking; otherwise they seem to stretch out beyond arm's length when it's time to eat. If you serve this with Chicken and Cabbage Salad, your daily vegetable quota will be met. If you are not making the salad and want your daily greens here, toss in a double handful of shredded napa cabbage, spinach, edamame beans, or frozen peas shortly before serving. Your *mien ga* will become a perfect little meal.

About ¼ pound dried bean thread noodles
(2 small packets; about 2 cups)

4 cups chicken broth

2 cups water

½ pound boneless chicken breasts or thighs, or ¾ pound bone-in chicken pieces

2 tablespoons fish sauce

½ teaspoon salt

½ teaspoon black pepper

2 tablespoons thinly sliced green onion

2 tablespoons coarsely chopped fresh cilantro

Place the tight, wiry bundles of bean thread noodles in a medium bowl and add warm water to cover. Let them soften until pliable, 10 to 20 minutes.

Meanwhile, in a medium saucepan, bring the broth and water to a boil over medium-high heat. Add the chicken, return to a boil, and then adjust the heat to maintain a lively simmer. Cook until the chicken is done, about 10 minutes. Transfer the chicken to a plate to cool. Add the fish sauce and salt to the broth and set aside.

When the chicken is cool enough to handle, tear it or chop it into bite-sized shreds and set aside. Drain the noodles well, transfer to a cutting board, and cut into 6-inch lengths.

To serve the *mien ga,* bring the broth to a boil, stir in the noodles, and cook until they swell and become shiny and clear, 1 to 2 minutes. Stir in the chicken, pepper, green onion, and cilantro, transfer to a serving bowl, and serve hot or warm in individual bowls, with a fork or chopsticks and a spoon.

SERVES 4

BEAN THREAD NOODLES STIR-FRIED WITH SHRIMP

mien xao tom

Bean thread noodles absorb seasonings exceptionally well: they deliver an abundance of flavor in a delicate way. Perfect with seafood and fresh herbs, they soften quickly and cook fast. Look for small, 1- to 2-ounce packets combined into a larger string sack, and keep them on your pantry shelf between the cereal and the spaghetti. Once softened, cut these noodles into 3-inch lengths; otherwise, they will be difficult to stir-fry and unwilling to mingle with their fellow ingredients. If you like, substitute fresh or canned crabmeat for the shrimp and you will have *mien xao cua*.

- **¼ pound dried bean thread noodles** (2 small packets; about 2 cups)
- **2 tablespoons vegetable oil**
- **1 tablespoon coarsely chopped garlic**
- **2 tablespoons coarsely chopped shallots**
- **10 to 12 medium shrimp, peeled and deveined, or ½ pound cooked crabmeat**
- **¾ cup chicken broth**
- **2 tablespoons fish sauce**
- **1 tablespoon soy sauce**
- **½ teaspoon pepper**
- **2 tablespoons thinly sliced green onion**
- **2 tablespoons coarsely chopped fresh cilantro**

Soften the bean thread noodles in warm water to cover until pliable, 10 to 15 minutes. Drain the noodles, line them up on a cutting board in a long pile, and cut crosswise into 3-inch lengths. Place all the ingredients by the stove: this stir-fry comes together fast.

In a large, heavy skillet or a wok, heat the oil over medium-high heat until a bit of garlic sizzles at once. Add the garlic and shallots and toss until fragrant and shiny. Add the shrimp and cook until bright pink on one side, 1 minute. (If using crabmeat, add with the green onions at the end of cooking.) Turn the shrimp to cook the other side, and then add the noodles. Cook for 1 minute and then toss again.

Add the broth, fish sauce, soy sauce, and pepper, and cook, tossing often, until the noodles are clear and tender and the shrimp are done, 3 to 5 minutes. Add a little more broth or a little more oil if the noodles stick.

Add the green onion and cilantro, toss once more, and transfer to a serving platter. Serve hot, warm, or at room temperature.

BUN THANG NOODLES

bun thang

Use leftover roast chicken and pork along with cold cuts from the deli for this fast feast. For a more traditional version, season the soup with 3 tablespoons dried shrimp and 2 teaspoons Asian-style shrimp paste, and top each serving with freshly squeezed lime juice.

½ pound dried rice noodles, linguine-width or thin threads

2 teaspoons vegetable oil

2 eggs, well beaten with 1 teaspoon fish sauce

6 cups chicken broth

2 tablespoons fish sauce

2 teaspoons sugar

1 teaspoon salt

1 ¼ cups thinly sliced cooked chicken

1 ¼ cups thinly sliced Vietnamese pâté such as *cha lua,* or cold cuts such as mortadella or baloney

1 ¼ cups thinly sliced roast pork, or ham

⅓ cup thinly sliced green onions

½ cup coarsely chopped fresh cilantro

Add the rice noodles to a medium saucepan of boiling water. Remove from heat and let stand 10 minutes. Drain, rinse with cold water, drain well, and set aside.

For omelet shreds, heat the oil in a large skillet for 1 minute over medium-high heat. Add the egg, swirl to coat the pan evenly, and cook until set and lightly browned, 1 to 2 minutes. Transfer to a cutting board, cool, and cut into thin strips.

To serve, combine the chicken broth, fish sauce, sugar, and salt in a medium saucepan over medium-high heat and bring to a rolling boil. Divide the noodles among 4 large Asian-style noodle soup bowls. Top each noodle serving with 4 equal piles of egg, chicken, Vietnamese pâté, and pork. Pour 1 ½ cups hot soup into each bowl, top with chopped green onions and cilantro, and serve at once with a big spoon for soup and chopsticks or forks for the noodles.

SWEETS & DRINKS

In Vietnam, sweets, puddings and other confections delight everyone: tiny children, stylish urban youth, civil servants, and white-haired elders. Sweets rule from dawn to bedtime. Eaten with spoons, out of hand, or sipped from straws, they are relished at bus stops, in school yards, and in chic sidewalk cafés. Sweet foods are far too important to Vietnamese people to be confined to a niche, like "desserts."

Try some of the sweet offerings at Asian markets when you go shopping for ingredients or cookware. Like the *cho,* or fresh markets, in Hanoi, Hoi An, Cantho, or Nha Trang, your local Asian market probably sells an array of sweet puddings, cakes, candies, and the unique Vietnamese pudding drink made with pearl tapioca beans, corn, and coconut milk. If you would like to try your hand at the inviting and rewarding repertoire of sweet things made the Vietnamese way, here are a number of treats you can cook up at home.

The first three recipes are sweet, delicious puddings that could also be described as soups or stews if you can put aside your Western views that soup should be savory. They are all very easy to make, and a great pleasure to have on hand for a cold morning's breakfast, a comforting midnight snack, or a potluck contribution sure to please little kids as well as big ones.

Next comes Crème Caramel (page 145), a souvenir of the time when France ruled much of Indochine from its colonial beachhead in Vietnam. This can be made richer with coconut milk, half-and-half, or extra egg yolks, depending on how luscious you like your custard. Vietnamese delis and takeout shops sell this delicious item unmolded into portable containers—a practical solution to the challenge of making something fragile available to go.

Sweet Coconut Ribbons, or *mut dua* (page 148), represent the candied fruits and nuts prepared at home or purchased in time to celebrate Tet, the lunar New Year festival, which occurs at the new moon between January and February. It is a celebration of Vietnamese family and culture, during which life slows down and families and friends gather to reflect, renew, rejoice, and eat lots of good things, including sweets like *mut dua.*

Finish your tour of Vietnam's sweet treats with three delicious things to drink: Fresh Lemongrass Tea (page 151), Fresh Soy Milk (page 152), and freshly brewed Vietnamese Coffee, Iced or Hot (page 154). Lemongrass tea is quickly brewed, and a good way to use leftover lemongrass (but go ahead and buy some to make this pleasing tea if there is none in your refrigerator). Cold or hot, sweet or not, it makes a lovely infusion with the power to calm one down in the most gentle way. Fresh Soy Milk isn't difficult to make, just a little messy. I enjoy the process when I'm not in a rush, and I revel in the nourishing taste of warm soy milk when it is ready.

Finally there are *ca-phé sua* and *ca-phé sua da,* the fabulous Vietnamese take on coffee with sweetened condensed milk, hot or iced. Glorious for those who love coffee, of whom I am one. If you, too, love coffee sweet and strong, indulge yourself in a *phin pha ca-phé,* the tiny, top-hat-shaped metal coffee filters of Vietnam. Make yourself a cup of *ca-phé sua da,* and sip it while you browse your way through this book. It's a time-out for grownups, since the coffee drips on its own timetable rather than yours. Stare out the window, call your faraway friend or sibling, or make a grocery list if you must multitask! Sweet, very sweet.

SERVES 8 TO 10

WARM BANANA-COCONUT PUDDING WITH TAPIOCA PEARLS

che chuoi

This is comfort food in any language, lovely for breakfast on a cold morning, or anytime you crave something soothing and sweet. Traditionally *che chuoi* is served warm. Its texture is more like a sweet stew than a thick, Western-style pudding. In Vietnam, cooks use a petite, sturdy variety of banana, which simmers for a while in the sauce. I use big ripe bananas from the grocery store and add them right before the pudding is ready, since they are already quite tender and sweet. I like to serve all the bananas right away, even if I have pudding leftover. When I serve the leftover pudding the next day, I warm it gently and add a fresh batch of bananas. If you love this as I do, try it with chunks of cooked sweet potatoes or *kabocha* pumpkin, or fresh or frozen corn. *Che chuoi* is often served with a sprinkling of chopped peanuts or toasted sesame seeds on top.

3 cups water

⅓ cup very small tapioca pearls

3 to 4 bananas

1½ cups unsweetened coconut milk (one 14-ounce can)

½ cup sugar

⅛ teaspoon salt

Bring the water to a rolling boil in a medium saucepan over high heat. Sprinkle in the tapioca, stirring the water so that it whirls around in the pan. Stir well for another minute or so to prevent the tapioca from clumping. Adjust the heat to maintain a lively simmer and cook, stirring often, until the tapioca pearls are clear except for their tiny white centers, about 10 minutes. Meanwhile, peel the bananas, halve them lengthwise and then crosswise, and then cut crosswise into 1-inch chunks. Set aside about 2 cups (and nibble the rest).

When the tapioca has softened, add the coconut milk, sugar, and salt, stirring well to dissolve the sugar. Add the bananas, cook for another 1 to 2 minutes, and remove from the heat. Serve hot or warm.

COCONUT PUDDING WITH STICKY RICE AND BLACK-EYED PEAS

che dau

I make this pudding with canned or frozen black-eyed peas, which I stir into the pudding in time to heat them up. This spares me the steps of soaking them and cooking them; too much trouble when all I want is a lovely little stirred and simmered pudding. This batch makes enough for a wintry afternoon snack, with plenty left over for breakfast later in the week.

½ cup long-grain sticky rice or long-grain rice

3 ½ cups water

¾ cup unsweetened coconut milk

½ cup canned or frozen black-eyed peas or corn, or cubes of cooked butternut squash, *kabocha* pumpkin, or sweet potato

½ cup sugar

Generous pinch of salt

Put the rice in a medium saucepan, add water to cover, swirl to rinse it well, and then drain. Add the 3 ½ cups of water, place over medium heat, and bring to a boil. Adjust the heat to maintain a gentle simmer and cook until the rice swells and softens, 10 to 15 minutes. Add the coconut milk, black-eyed peas, sugar, and salt, and stir well. Cook for 2 to 3 minutes to dissolve the sugar and mix everything thoroughly. Remove from the heat, let stand for 10 to 15 minutes, and serve warm or at room temperature. Or cover and refrigerate for up to 2 days, and reheat gently just before serving time.

SERVES 6 TO 8

BLACK STICKY RICE PUDDING

xoi nep than dua

The velvety purple color of this sweet, satisfying dish is almost as delicious as the pudding itself. At my house we love it just like this, but if we have extra coconut milk or half-and-half handy, we crown each serving with a little splash, just to enjoy the contrast with that purple, before we dig in. You will find *xoi nep,* or black sticky rice, in many Asian markets or through mail-order sources (page 162). Its plump black grains are dappled with white and brown, offering no hint of the purple waiting to emerge as it cooks. Like white sticky rice, it is high in amylopectin, the starch that causes rice grains to cling together when cooked. Because it is a brown, or whole-grain rice, it needs a little more cooking time than polished white rice.

1 ½ cups black sticky rice

3 cups water

½ cup unsweetened coconut milk

⅓ cup sugar

½ teaspoon salt

Put the rice in a medium bowl, add water to cover the rice by at least 2 inches, and soak for at least 3 hours and up to 12 hours.

Drain the rice well and transfer to a medium saucepan. Add the 3 cups of water, stir well, and bring to a lively boil over medium-high heat. Reduce the heat to maintain a very gentle boil, and let the rice cook for 30 minutes, stirring well now and then. Meanwhile, combine the coconut milk, sugar, and salt in a small saucepan and bring to a gentle boil. Stir well to dissolve the sugar and salt, and set aside.

When the rice has cooked for 30 minutes, reduce the heat to low and cook until shiny, tender, plump, and a gorgeous purple hue, about 10 minutes. It will still have the pleasingly rustic texture of brown rice, rather than that of polished white rice.

Remove the rice from the heat, mix in the warm coconut sauce, and stir well. Transfer the pudding to a serving bowl and serve hot, warm, or at room temperature in small bowls. Or cover and refrigerate the cooled pudding for up to 3 days, reheating gently just before serving time.

SERVES 8

CRÈME CARAMEL

banh ca ra men

Sweet and luscious custard enjoyed favor in Vietnam and throughout Southeast Asia long before French cuisine arrived on the scene. Made with coconut milk, duck eggs, and palm sugar, it was steamed rather than baked in a bain-marie, or water bath. The classic French *crème renversée au caramel* quickly found favor when French rule came to Vietnam, and was part of the country's culinary repertoire by the time the colonial era came to an end. Some versions of *banh ca ra men* are enriched by a combination of milk and coconut milk, or several egg yolks in addition to whole eggs. You will need 8 custard cups or ½-cup ramekins, or small ovenproof glass bowls.

FOR THE CARAMEL

¾ cup sugar

½ cup water

FOR THE CUSTARD

5 eggs

¾ cup sugar

3 cups milk

To prepare the caramel, place the custard cups by the stove, ready to receive a dollop of hot caramel as soon as it's ready. In a heavy, medium saucepan, combine the sugar and water and cook over medium heat, tilting the pan to swirl the liquid until the sugar dissolves and combines with the water to make a clear syrup, about 5 minutes. Increase the heat to medium-high and gently boil the syrup, lifting and tilting the pan now and then to cook it evenly, until the syrup turns golden, then light brown, and suddenly a whiskey or tea color. Quickly and carefully pour the caramel into the custard cups, dividing it evenly among them. Set the pan aside and tilt each cup to coax the caramel to cover the bottom. Don't worry if it is uneven; it will all cook together into a beautiful crown. Set aside.

Preheat the oven to 350°F. To prepare the custard, in a medium bowl, whisk or beat the eggs until foamy and then add the sugar. Beat well to dissolve the sugar, add the milk, and beat until well combined. Pour the custard into the custard cups, place them in

continued

a baking or roasting pan, and add enough water to come halfway up the sides of the cups. Place in the oven and bake until the custard is firm around the edges and fairly set in the center, and the tip of a knife stuck in the center comes out clean, 40 to 50 minutes. Remove from the oven, carefully remove the cups from the pan of hot water, and place on a cooling rack. Cover and chill if serving time is more than 1 hour away, for up to 2 days.

Serve at room temperature or chilled. Very gently, loosen the edges of each custard with a table knife. Place a small serving plate upside down over the custard cup, and invert the cup so that the custard drops onto the plate, displaying its dark, caramel-infused crown and releasing a small pool of thin, delicious sauce.

MAKES ABOUT 2 CUPS OF COCONUT RIBBONS

SWEET COCONUT RIBBONS

mut dua

The lunar New Year celebration known in Vietnam as Tet is a time of remembering the past and envisioning the coming year. In hopes of a sweet year ahead, filled with prosperity, harmony, health, and all-around good luck, people set aside quarrels and worries and focus on all things happy and good. Eating is central to the celebration, and sweets are a ubiquitous treat during Tet, symbolizing the wish for life's sweetest pleasures throughout the coming year. Typical offerings include candied fruits, nuts, and seeds. This sweet coconut treat is a delicious example.

You can use a fresh coconut, or make it with wide strips or flakes of dried coconut, available in many health-food stores. I use a vegetable peeler to shred the coconut meat into thin ribbons, each about 2 inches long. To do this, hold a chunk of coconut firmly in one hand over a plate, and shave strips off its curved edge. Stop when a chunk shrinks enough in size to bring the peeler close to your fingers. (You can save the small chunks in the refrigerator or freezer until you have enough to grate for a dessert.) Or shred the coconut meat with a food processor fitted with the slicing disk. This is faster, but the shreds come out thicker and less pliable than hand-shredded coconut. Either way, you should have about 2 cups of shredded coconut.

¾ cup sugar

½ teaspoon salt

¼ cup water

4 cups large, freshly pared coconut chunks or wide strips or flakes of dried coconut

Combine the sugar, salt, and water in a heavy-bottomed, medium saucepan. Bring to a gentle boil over medium heat. Add the coconut ribbons, lower the heat to maintain a gentle simmer, and cook, stirring often and coating the ribbons with the gradually reducing and thickening syrup.

continued

Once the syrup forms large bubbles and begins to crystallize on the sides of the pot, stir constantly with a fork to keep the ribbons separate and moving around, until the syrup dries up completely into dry, white grains. Turn out the ribbons onto a platter, pulling apart any clumps so they cool and dry evenly. Serve warm or at room temperature. Or cool completely and store in a tightly sealed glass jar.

NOTE: Opening a fresh coconut is quick and easy once you know how, but it can be an intimidating prospect to people raised far from tropical climes. My shortcut method is this: Equip yourself with a hammer and a towel that can survive a good splash of clear, sweet coconut juice, and take these, along with a hairy, brown coconut heavy with juice, outside to a hard, flat surface, such as a corner of your backyard. Wrap the coconut in the towel and place it on the ground, arranging the towel to keep it from rolling about. Squat down, take a deep breath, and strike it with a mighty blow. Try again, until the coconut cracks open, releasing its juice. Now back to the kitchen, where you can pry the white, firm meat away from the hard, brown shell with a table knife, and proceed to use the coconut meat according to your needs.

FRESH LEMONGRASS TEA

tra xa

Cooking Vietnamese food puts you "up close and personal" with the ethereal herb known in English as lemongrass, and in Vietnamese as *xa*. If you love its aroma and flavor as I do, you will enjoy this simple and beautiful tea, made with fresh lemongrass stalks.

4 cups water

6 stalks fresh lemongrass

¼ to ⅓ cup sugar

In a medium saucepan, bring the water to a lively boil over medium-high heat. Meanwhile, prepare the lemongrass: trim 1 inch off the grassy top and pare away any dried root portion at the base, leaving a smooth end below the bulb. Remove any dried, sad-looking outer leaves as well. Cut each stalk diagonally into 1-inch pieces to expose its purple-tinged, aromatic core. You should have about 2 cups.

When the water boils, add the lemongrass and sugar and stir well. Adjust the heat to maintain a gentle boil, and simmer for 5 minutes. Remove from the heat, cover, and let the tea steep for at least 10 minutes.

To serve hot, strain the tea into cups or a teapot. To serve cold, leave the lemongrass chunks steeping in the tea as it cools to room temperature. Strain the cooled tea, transfer to a pitcher, and serve over ice. The tea will keep in the refrigerator for up to 2 days.

SERVES 2; MAKES ABOUT 2 CUPS OF SOYMILK

FRESH SOY MILK

sua dau nanh

I love the taste of freshly made soy milk, and I enjoy making it as a treat. Do it when you are not in a hurry, as it involves advance preparation (soaking the soybeans for at least 6 hours), and a straightforward but messy middle step (puréeing the soaked beans and straining them well). The third and final step is short and sweet: simmering the soy milk briefly until its raw, beany aroma softens to a sweet, smooth scent and flavor. Then it is ready to sip, sweeten, or infuse with lemongrass, fresh ginger, or another flavor you like. You can buy dried whole soybeans in most Asian markets and in many health-food stores. They are hard, dry, a beautiful café au lait brown in color, and about the size of green peas. A good supply of cheesecloth is a plus for making soy milk, but you can use kitchen towels instead.

⅔ cup whole dried soybeans

3 cups water

Combine the soybeans and water in a bowl and set aside to soak for 6 to 8 hours. The soybeans will triple in size and swell to an oval shape. When you're ready to make the soy milk, set out a medium saucepan, a large spoon, and a fine-mesh strainer. (You could also use a medium bowl lined with several layers of cheesecloth or a clean kitchen towel.)

Put about half the soybeans and the water in the jar of a blender and process to a fairly smooth purée, pulsing on and off as needed. Place the strainer over the saucepan and pour in the purée. Use the spoon to press the soybean purée against the strainer to extract as much liquid as possible. Repeat with the remaining soybeans and water. Or pour the purée into the bowl lined with cheesecloth or a kitchen towel in small batches, gathering the cheesecloth and squeezing gently but diligently to extract as much liquid as possible. Transfer to the saucepan. Place the saucepan over medium-high heat and bring the soy milk to a gentle boil. Reduce the heat to low and simmer, stirring often, until the aroma changes from "beany" to a fresh, sweet scent, about 10 minutes.

Remove from the heat and serve hot or warm, or cool to room temperature, chill, and serve cold. The soy milk will keep for 1 or 2 days in the refrigerator.

SERVES 1

VIETNAMESE COFFEE, ICED OR HOT

ca-phé sua da; ca-phé sua

Vietnamese coffee is a lingering souvenir of the French colonial presence in Vietnam. Along with delicious baguettes and the fabulous sandwiches they inspired, *ca-phé sua da* long ago made itself at home, embraced with such passion that it has become something very Vietnamese. You can make it at home with ease, with or without the signature top-hat contraption used to prepare *ca-phé* in Vietnamese establishments. You'll find them in many Asian markets and through mail-order sources (page 162), along with a supply of coffee: look for Café du Monde, in the curry-colored cans from New Orleans, and the imported Trung Nguyên Coffee, in the handsome red cans, made with coffee beans grown in Vietnam. If you lack the metal filter but long for the taste, pour 2 tablespoons of sweetened condensed milk into a coffee cup or sturdy bistro glass. Brew some espresso, add it to the cup, and stir like crazy. Voilà *ca-phé sua!* Pour over ice and it's *ca-phé sua da.*

2 tablespoons sweetened condensed milk

2 tablespoons finely ground dark-roast coffee

¾ cup boiling water

Spoon the sweetened condensed milk into a coffee cup or a short drinking glass and place the Vietnamese coffee filter on top of it. For iced coffee, fill a tall glass with ice cubes and set aside. Remove the coffee filter's lid, unscrew the inner press, and set both aside. Add the ground coffee, and then screw the press lightly in place to pack the coffee down a bit. Add the boiling water, cover with the lid, and let the water drip through the coffee, 3 to 5 minutes.

Remove the lid and rest it upside down. Then place the drained filter basket on the inverted lid to catch any last drops of coffee. Stir well to mix the coffee with the milk. For iced coffee, pour the coffee into the ice-filled glass, and serve. For hot coffee, skip the glass of ice, or *da,* and sip (carefully) your steaming *ca-phé sua.*

SAUCES & OTHER BASIC RECIPES

Here are your paints and brushes—an array of simple, flavorful condiments, components, and finishing touches with which to complete your Vietnamese dishes. Everyday Dipping Sauce (this page) is just that, an incomparable, delicate sauce that appears throughout the repertoire of Vietnamese dishes, from spring rolls and fritters to grilled meatballs, enormous bowls of rice noodles, table-top fondue feasts, and simple country meals of rice and fish. You can make it in a traditional mortar, in a mini–food processor or a blender, or with a knife and a spoon. It is marvelous. Made with surprisingly simple ingredients, it complements and brings harmony to the cuisine of Vietnam.

You'll also find numerous other sauces, each with a particular traditional use, but tasty on its own. The remaining recipes include Ginger-Lime Dipping Sauce (facing page), Lime-Pepper-Salt Dipping Sauce (page 158), and Caramel Sauce (page 158), a simple syrup used to color and flavor simmered dishes. Only Everyday Dipping Sauce or Vegetarian Dipping Sauce (facing page) is essential; the remaining recipes are rewarding extras, a part of the big picture of cooking quick and easy Vietnamese food.

EVERYDAY DIPPING SAUCE *(NUOC CHAM)*

This traditional sauce appears on the table at most Vietnamese meals. Add a small handful of shredded carrots and you have a vegetable relish. For the ultimate *nuoc cham,* grind the garlic, chili, and sugar with a mortar and pestle. Or smash the garlic through a garlic press, or mince it finely and mash it with the sugar and chilies on the side of the bowl with the back of your spoon. Or simply stir it all together. As long as you dissolve the sugar, you will have a delicious sauce.

1 tablespoon chopped garlic

2 tablespoons sugar

½ teaspoon chili-garlic sauce or finely chopped fresh hot red chilies, or 1 teaspoon dried red chili flakes

3 tablespoons fish sauce

3 tablespoons water

2 tablespoons freshly squeezed lime juice

Combine the garlic, sugar, and chili-garlic sauce in the bowl of a mortar and mash to a paste. (Or combine them on your cutting board and mash to a coarse paste with a fork and the back of a spoon.) Scrape the paste into a small bowl and stir in the fish sauce, water, and lime juice. Stir well to dissolve the sugar. Transfer to small serving bowls for dipping. Or transfer to a jar, cover, and refrigerate for up to 1 week.

Makes about ½ cup

VEGETARIAN EVERYDAY DIPPING SAUCE *(NUOC CHAM CHAY)*

Many Vietnamese dishes are seasoned in expectation that they will be served with *nuoc cham* or another flavorful table sauce. This sauce doesn't re-create *nuoc cham,* but it does provide a delicious vegetarian accompaniment to vegetarian versions of Summer Rolls (page 31), grilled vegetables, tofu, noodle dishes, and rice. It tastes great to non-vegetarians as well, and keeps, covered and refrigerated, for up to 5 days.

¼ cup soy sauce

¼ cup freshly squeezed lime juice or white vinegar

¼ cup pineapple juice

¼ cup fresh or canned pineapple chunks

3 tablespoons sugar

2 teaspoons Asian sesame oil

2 teaspoons salt

2 tablespoons coarsely chopped fresh cilantro

1 tablespoon coarsely chopped garlic

¼ teaspoon chili-garlic sauce, chopped fresh hot chilies, dried red chili flakes, or other hot sauce

Combine all the ingredients in a mini–food processor or a blender and blend until smooth. Serve in small bowls at room temperature, or cover and refrigerate for up to 5 days.

Makes about ⅔ cup

GINGER-LIME DIPPING SAUCE *(NUOC MAM GUNG)*

The fabulous flavor of this classic sauce lights up simple poached and grilled foods, such as Hainan Chicken and Rice (page 60), grilled or boiled shrimp, or grilled salmon or tuna. It's also terrific with a simple platter of grilled or oven-roasted vegetables.

2 tablespoons chopped fresh ginger

2 teaspoons chopped garlic

3 tablespoons sugar

½ teaspoon salt

3 tablespoons fish sauce

3 tablespoons freshly squeezed lime juice

2 tablespoons water

½ teaspoon chili-garlic sauce, dried red chili flakes, or chopped fresh hot chilies

Combine all the ingredients in a blender or mini–food processor, and blend until you have a fairly smooth sauce. Transfer to a small bowl, stir to be sure the sugar has dissolved, and set aside until serving time. Or combine the ginger, garlic, sugar, and salt in the bowl of a mortar and grind to a grainy paste. Transfer to a medium bowl and add the fish sauce, lime juice, water, and chili-garlic sauce, stirring until the sugar is dissolved and the sauce is fairly smooth. Pour the sauce into small serving bowls. Or transfer to a jar, cover tightly, and store in the refrigerator for up to 1 week.

Makes about ½ cup

LIME-PEPPER-SALT DIPPING SAUCE *(MUOI TIEU CHANH)*

This little condiment displays the Vietnamese genius with seasonings. Three bold ingredients, arranged in a small bowl, are kept apart until showtime, then stirred together by the diner for a wonderful condiment. The lime-pepper-salt mixture shows up in Chicken Curry with Sweet Potatoes (page 56) and Shaking Beef with Purple Onions and Watercress (page 72) and is also delicious with steamed clams or mussels, grilled or boiled shrimp, and fried rice. Traditionally it's presented as a single diner's condiment, but since you may be serving a crowd of hungry folks floating around the buffet table, I've given a variation for a shared portion.

½ teaspoon salt

½ teaspoon black pepper

1 wedge of lime (about ⅙ of a whole lime)

Mound the salt on one side of a saucer and the pepper on the other, leaving the center free for the wedge of lime. Let each guest squeeze the lime juice into the center and then stir, coaxing the three flavors into a thick little spot of sauce. Enjoy with grilled, roasted, or fried food.

A Bowl for Sharing:

In a small bowl, combine 2 tablespoons of salt, 2 tablespoons of black pepper, and ½ cup of freshly squeezed lime juice (2 or 3 limes) and stir well to dissolve the seasonings into the lime juice. Transfer to a small serving bowl. Guests can spoon the sauce onto their food or onto their plates, or use it for dipping.

Makes ½ cup

CARAMEL SAUCE FOR SEASONING SAVORY DISHES *(NUOC MAU)*

Making caramel is the kitchen paradox—it can be very easy, but also very easily botched. The sugar seems to be caramelizing as slowly as molasses in January, and then, just when you lose patience and step over to the sink for a tiny sip of water, it starts smoking and changing color very fast. Making this sauce is a lesson in patience and focus (areas in which I can always find room to improve). Caramel Sauce is used in a number of Vietnamese dishes because of its handsome color and rich flavor note, but it is not essential to creating a wonderful dish. If you don't want to make this sauce, you can substitute an equal amount of brown sugar for the Caramel Sauce in any recipe, or make the Brown Sugar Sauce (following).

¼ cup cold water

¾ cup sugar

¼ cup hot water

Combine the cold water and sugar in a sturdy, medium saucepan over medium-high heat and stir well. Cook, tilting the pan to swirl the sauce now and then until the liquid becomes syrupy and the color begins to change, 5 to 7 minutes. Have the hot water handy by the stove.

Watch carefully as soon as the syrup turns from clear to soft gold, to the color of honey. Swirl the syrup gently now and then, and be vigilant; this is the point at which things start to happen fast. When the syrup is as dark as maple syrup, but not as dark as molasses, carefully pour the hot water down the side of the saucepan, and expect a small eruption of bubbling, steamy chaos.

Once the syrup settles down, continue cooking, stirring, until you have a smooth, thin, and handsome caramel-colored sauce.

Set aside to cool, and then transfer to a jar and close tightly. The syrup will keep at room temperature for up to 1 month.

Makes about 1 cup

Brown Sugar Sauce:

For a quick, simple substitute for Caramel Sauce, combine ¾ cup of brown sugar and ¾ cup of water in a medium saucepan. Bring to a boil over medium-high heat, adjust the heat to maintain a lively simmer, and cook until you have a dark, rich syrup, 5 to 10 minutes. Cool and store in a tightly sealed jar for up to 1 month.

TANGY BROWN BEAN DIPPING DAUCE *(TUONG GOI CUON)*

This pungent sauce traditionally accompanies Summer Rolls with Shrimp and Mint (page 31) and Sugarcane Shrimp (page 27). It happens to be vegetarian, and goes nicely with grilled or roasted food. Be sure to try the variation that follows, Hoisin-Peanut Dipping Sauce. Hoisin sauce is a sweeter, darker first cousin of brown bean sauce. Available in many supermarkets as well as Asian groceries, it combines well with peanuts to make a delicious sauce.

FOR THE SAUCE

½ cup unsweetened coconut milk

⅔ cup water

⅓ cup brown bean sauce, also called ground bean sauce

1 tablespoon white vinegar

2 tablespoons peanut butter or finely ground roasted and salted peanuts

2 tablespoons sugar

1 tablespoon minced shallot or onion

GARNISHES

1 or 2 tablespoons chili-garlic sauce or any hot sauce

2 tablespoons chopped roasted and salted peanuts

To prepare the sauce, combine all the ingredients in a small saucepan and bring to a boil over medium-high heat. Adjust the heat to maintain a gentle simmer and cook, stirring now and then, until the sugar and peanut butter dissolve and you have a fairly smooth sauce, 3 to 5 minutes. Cool to room temperature, and serve in small bowls, each garnished with a dollop of chili-garlic sauce and a sprinkling of peanuts. Or transfer to a jar, cover, and refrigerate for up to 5 days.

Makes about ¾ cup

Hoisin-Peanut Dipping Sauce:

Sweeter than the main recipe, this will complement any grilled or roasted dish as well as Summer Rolls. Substitute ⅓ cup of hoisin sauce for the brown bean sauce and proceed with the recipe.

Quick & Easy Vietnamese Menus

Breakfast Special

Omelet with Crabmeat and Green Onions (page 59)

Warm baguette with butter and jam

Vietnamese Coffee, Hot (page 154)

A Northern Feast

Grilled Pork Patties with Lettuce, Noodles, Peanuts, and Mint, Hanoi Style (page 76)

Cha Ca Fish with Fresh Dill, Hanoi Style (page 89)

Sticky Rice with Mung Beans, Northern Style (page 120)

Chinese tea with butter cookies

A Southern Feast

Hu Tieu Noodles with Pork and Shrimp, Saigon Style (page 131)

Pork in Caramel Sauce (page 80)

Everyday Rice (page 116)

Everyday Herb and Salad Plate (page 100)

Fresh pineapple, ripe melon, or grapes

Beach Weekend

Crab and Asparagus Soup (page 50)

Lemongrass Shrimp (page 26)

Grilled Tuna Steaks with Pineapple-Chili Sauce (page 84)

Lime sorbet and wonderful chocolates

Streamlined Seven Course Beef

Shaking Beef with Purple Onions and Watercress (page 72)

Grilled Leaf-Wrapped Beef Kebabs (page 33)

Vietnamese Meat Loaf (page 75)

Delicious Lemongrass Burgers with Beef (page 71)

Big, Cool Noodle Bowl without meat (page 133)

Everyday Dipping Sauce (page 156)

Classic Chicken Combo

Chicken and Cabbage Salad with Fresh Mint (page 102)

Bean Thread Noodles with Chicken (page 137)

Bread Sticks

Lemonade

Fish and Seafood Feast

Salmon Steaks in Caramel Fish Sauce (page 96)

Sweet and Tangy Soup with Pineapple, Tamarind, and Shrimp (page 48)

Everyday Rice (page 116)

Lemon and lime sorbet

Too Hot to Cook

Big, Cool Noodle Bowl with Roast Chicken, Cucumbers, and Mint (page 133)

Thickly sliced tomato sprinkled with salt and pepper

Fresh Lemongrass Tea (page 151) over ice

Ice cream with summer berries

Too Cold to Go Out

Meatball Soup (page 42), with spinach leaves

Crusty bread with cheddar or Jack cheese

Black Sticky Rice Pudding (page 144), with cream

A Busy Day Rice Plate *(COM DIA)*

(For when you have everything but the fried egg left over from other feasts.)

Omelet with Bean Thread Noodles and Pork (page 65)

Grilled Garlic-Pepper Pork Chops (page 79)

Everyday Rice (page 116)

Everyday Dipping Sauce (page 156)

Fried egg, over easy

Shredded lettuce, sliced tomato, and cucumber

Tailgate Picnic, or Campout Supper with a Twist

Summer Rolls with Shrimp and Mint (page 31)

Submarine Sandwiches, Saigon Style (page 38)

Apples and grapes

Trail mix

Vietnamese Coffee, Iced (page 154)

Blondies and brownies

MAIL-ORDER SOURCES

Ingredients and Utensils

Adriana's Caravan

43rd Street and Lexington Avenue
New York, NY 10017
(800) 316-0820
www.adrianascaravan.com

Import Food

P.O. BOX 2054
Issaquah, WA 98027
(888) 618-8424; fax (425) 687-8413
www.importfood.com

Temple of Thai

P.O. BOX 112
Carroll, IA 51401
(877) 811-8773; fax (712) 792-0698
www.templeofthai.com

Asian Herbs, Plants, and Seeds

Lazy Susan Ranch

P.O. BOX 1152
Calistoga, CA 94515
(707) 942-0120
www.lazysusanranch.com

Nichols Garden Nursery

190 North Pacific Highway
Albany, OR 97321
(503) 928-9280
www.gardennursery.com

Richters Herbs

357 Highway 47
Goodwood, ON L0C 1A0
Canada
(905) 640-6677
www.richters.com

Sandy Mush Herbs Nursery

316 Surrett Cove Road
Leicester, NC 28748
(828) 683-2014
www.sandymushherbs.com

Southern Exposure Seed Exchange

P.O. BOX 460
Mineral, VA 23117
(540) 894-9480; fax (540) 894-9481
www.southernexposure.com

Books & Resources on the Food and Cooking of Southeast Asia and Vietnam

Alford, Jeffrey, and Naomi Duguid. *Hot, Sour, Salty, Sweet.* New York: Artisan, 2000.

Bladholm, Linda. *The Asian Grocery Store Demystified: A Food Lover's Guide to All the Best Ingredients.* Los Angeles: Renaissance Books, 1999.

Carmack, Robert, Didier Corlou, and Thanh Van Nguyen. *Vietnamese Home Cooking.* Boston: Periplus Editions, 1998.

Choi, Trieu Thi, Marcel Isaak, and Doling Jackson. *The Food of Vietnam: Authentic Recipes from the Heart of Indochina.* Boston: Periplus Editions, 2003.

Cost, Bruce. *Bruce Cost's Asian Ingredients.* New York: William Morrow, 1998.

Davidson, Alan. *Seafood of South-East Asia.* Singapore: Federal Publications, 1976.

Duong, Binh, and Marcia Kiesel. *Simple Art of Vietnamese Cooking.* New York: Prentice Hall, 1991.

Hongtong, Penn. *Simple Laotian Cooking.* New York: Hippocrene Books, 2003.

Jaffrey, Madhur. *Madhur Jaffrey's Far Eastern Cookery.* New York: Harper & Row, 1989.

———. *A Taste of the Far East.* New York: Crown, 1993.

Jue, Joyce. *Savoring Southeast Asia: Recipes and Reflections on Southeast Asian Cooking.* San Francisco: Weldon-Owen, 2000.

McDermott, Nancie. *Real Thai: The Best of Thailand's Regional Cooking.* San Francisco: Chronicle Books, 1992.

———. *Real Vegetarian Thai.* San Francisco: Chronicle Books, 1997.

Miller, Jill Nhu Hong. *Vietnamese Cookery.* Rutland, Vt.: Charles E. Tuttle, 1986.

Ngo, Bach, and Gloria Zimmerman. *The Classic Cuisine of Vietnam.* Woodbury, N.Y.: Barron's, 1979.

Nguyen, Chi, and Judy Monroe. *Cooking the Vietnamese Way.* Minneapolis, Minn.: Lerner Publications Company, 1979.

Pham, Mai. *The Best of Thai and Vietnamese Cooking.* Rooklin, Calif.: Prima Publishing, 1996.

———. *Pleasures of the Vietnamese Table.* New York: Harpercollins, 2001.

Routhier, Nicole. *The Foods of Vietnam.* New York: Stewart, Tabori & Chang, 1989.

Solomon, Charmaine. *The Complete Asian Cookbook.* New York: McGraw-Hill, 1985.

Sterling, Richard. *World Food: Vietnam.* Oakland, Calif.: Lonely Planet, 2000.

Stuart, Anh Thu. *Vietnamese Cooking: Recipes My Mother Taught Me.* London: Angus & Robertson, 1986.

Tran, Diana My. *The Vietnamese Cookbook.* Sterling, Va.: Capital Books, 2000.

Trang, Corrine. *Authentic Vietnamese Cooking: Food from a Family Table.* New York: Simon & Schuster, 1999.

———. *Essentials of Asian Cuisine: Fundamentals and Favorite Recipes.* New York: Simon & Schuster, 2003.

Web Site

Viet World Kitchen. http://www.vietworldkitchen.com. Andrea Nguyen's superb site on Vietnamese food and culinary traditions.

INDEX

Table of Equivalents

The exact equivalents in the following tables have been rounded for convenience.

LIQUID/DRY MEASURES

U.S.	Metric
¼ teaspoon	1.25 milliliters
½ teaspoon	2.5 milliliters
1 teaspoon	5 milliliters
1 tablespoon (3 teaspoons)	15 milliliters
1 fluid ounce (2 tablespoons)	30 milliliters
¼ cup	60 milliliters
⅓ cup	80 milliliters
½ cup	120 milliliters
1 cup	240 milliliters
1 pint (2 cups)	480 milliliters
1 quart (4 cups, 32 ounces)	960 milliliters
1 gallon (4 quarts)	3.84 liters
1 ounce (by weight)	28 grams
1 pound	454 grams
2.2 pounds	1 kilogram

LENGTH

U.S.	Metric
⅛ inch	3 millimeters
¼ inch	6 millimeters
½ inch	12 millimeters
1 inch	2.5 centimeters

OVEN TEMPERATURE

Fahrenheit	Celsius	Gas
250	**120**	**½**
275	**140**	**1**
300	**150**	**2**
325	**160**	**3**
350	**180**	**4**
375	**190**	**5**
400	**200**	**6**
425	**220**	**7**
450	**230**	**8**
475	**240**	**9**
500	**260**	**10**